ANY OTHER COUNTRY

EXCEPT MY OWN

HADLEY A. THOMAS

ANY OTHER COUNTRY

EXCEPT MY OWN

HADLEY A. THOMAS

Cross Cultural Publications, Inc.

CrossRoads Books

Published by **CROSS CULTURAL PUBLICATIONS, INC.**
CROSS ROADS BOOKS
Post Office Box 506
Notre Dame, Indiana, 46556, U.S.A.
Phone: (219) 272-0889
FAX: (219) 273-5973

ISBN: 0-940121-23-9
Library of Congress Catalog Card Number: 94-71045

To Helen, whose dedication
and encouragement made this
book possible.

ACKNOWLEDGEMENTS

There are many people who guided and assisted me during my tenure on the reservation. All of them shared their knowledge with me. Each one spent many hours answering questions and coaching me in protocol and the use of Navajo expressions to keep me from making the mistakes which non-Indians usually make when they move to the reservation.

The time at Red Rock was made enjoyable by the wonderful friendship of Troy and Edith Kennedy, the traders. They took us under their wings and helped us survive our first two years as newlyweds and new teachers.

Bertha Benally and Leslie Francisco taught us the traditions of visiting Navajo families in their hogans in the community. Bertha always taught me the male Navajo expressions so I didn't sound silly to the Navajo people. Leslie gave me his loyalty and dedication that was so needed to make a very rundown, neglected school look good.

Marie Yazzie at Wide Ruins kept me apprised of the community activities at Wide Ruins. Tribal Council Member Annie Wauneka supported our efforts at the school and later on in other endeavors.

Patrick Nataani was instrumental in completing an accurate census at Steamboat. He guided me in making responses to the children, parents and community members that led to successful educational practices.

Paul Williams, Tribal Council Member, coordinated the needs of the school and those of the community, spending many hours at this task.

Harry Isaac introduced me to the community at Tuba City. George Adson taught me more about living in the Navajo Community than anyone I know. He included me in his personal life. I enjoyed the fruits of his farm during different seasonal activities. We visited a Paiute camp and watched sing baskets being woven. He introduced me to important Navajo community people. When a respected Hatathlie became upset about a science class, George negotiated an amicable settlement of the problem. He was unmatched as a locator of truants.

Mr. Leo Denetdeal was my "Grandfather." He spent hours telling me the about the Navajo culture and beliefs. His silver haired head was always held high and his brown eyes sparkled as he told me of his boyhood experiences in a traditional Navajo home.

Joshua Kaya, a Hatathlie, taught me and the school children about the animals of the southwest and their place in the Navajo culture.

I must not forget to acknowledge Irvy Goosen for his friendship, as well as his kindness and patience in trying to make me functional in the Navajo language. I understand it better than I ever spoke it.

To the many others who made our life enjoyable because of their friendship and support, I give my heartfelt thanks.

October, 1993   Hadley A. Thomas

                                       Glendale, AZ

PREFACE

In 1951 my wife and I went to Arizona to teach Navajo children for one year. We remained on the reservation until 1972. This brief sojourn in the span of time made me forever impressed by this wonderful group of Americans.

During my years on the reservation I became aware that most Americans do not understand what reservations are or how they came to be. They do not understand the ramifications of Indian treaties, or the legal rights Indians derive from them. And people mostly do not understand the rich religious beliefs and history of Indians.

The historical information in this book is contained in documents available to those who care to pursue the research for the data. The conclusions and recommendations, where offered, are based upon the broad personal experience of the author and may differ from those of others. This book is an attempt to present data that will provide a better understanding of the Navajos and their heritage.

The reader will follow the impact of the Spanish, Mexican, other Indians, and Americans upon the culture of the Navajos. These people live on 24,000 square miles of rugged, semi-arid territory in the states of Arizona, Utah, and New Mexico. The area is approximately the size of West Virginia. They are the largest Indian tribe in the United States. They refer to themselves as the Navajo Nation because of the treaty with the government of the United States. Even though the Navajos have made tremendous strides into the American mainstream in recent years, their advancement has not been as great as that of non-Indian groups in education, health, employment, housing and other economical and social areas. They have maintained much of their cultural heritage in a rapidly changing era with increasing self-determination and economic pressure. Despite these pressures, there is an "inner-belief" that preserves the uniqueness of the Navajo people.

The continuing desire of the Navajos for their land was best expressed by the great headman Barboncito to General W. T. Sheridan of the United States Army at Bosque Redondo, New Mexico in 1868, when he said, *"I hope to God you will not ask me to go to any other country except my own!"*[1]

CONTENTS

TITLE	PAGE
Dedication	i
Acknowledgments	ii
Preface	iv
Chapter One: Dine Means, "The People"	1
Chapter Two: The Immigrants	21
Chapter Three: The Spaniards	33
Chapter Four: Rebellion and Change	44
Chapter Five: The Yankee Solution	55
Chapter Six: Conquest and Imprisonment	71
Chapter Seven: Return to a Reservation	88
Chapter Eight: Self Determination	101
Chapter Nine: A Classroom for Every Thirty Children	119
Chapter Ten: Continuing Problems of Education	134
Chapter Eleven: Reservation Livelihood	146
Chapter Twelve: Health Problems	159
Chapter Thirteen: Cultural Conflicts	169

Contents

(Continued)

TITLE	PAGE
Appendix A	189
Appendix B	223
Appendix C	225
Appendix D	228
Appendix E	232
Endnotes	233
Sources	248
Glossary of Navajo Terms	254
Index	257

MAPS

TITLE	PAGE
Map 1: The Four Sacred Mountains	13
Map 2: Pre-European Pueblo Settlements	30
Map 3: Native American Reservations	58
Map 4: Forts Around Navajo in 1864	72
Map 5: Reservation at Fort Sumner	77
Map 6: Reservation Growth	100

ILLUSTRATIONS

TITLE		PAGE
Illustration 1:	Sandpainting Animals	18
Illustration 2:	Sandpainting Plants	19
Illustration 3:	Pueblo Style Influence on Navajo Homes	48
Illustration 4:	Bosque Redondo	79
Illustration 5:	Navajo Camp After Imprisonment	90
Illustration 6:	Student and Workers at Fort Defiance before 1894	122
Illustration 7:	Students at Shiprock School	127

CHARTS

TITLE		PAGE
Chart 1:	Example of Translation	4
Chart 2:	Personal Pronouns	6
Chart 3:	Paradigm for a Verb Stem	9
Chart 4:	Treaties Between the United States and the Navajo Nation	87
Chart 5:	Navajo Tribal Chairmen	108
Chart 6:	Student Enrollment From 1950 to 1960	131

CHAPTER ONE

DINE MEANS, "THE PEOPLE"

When one begins to learn about a group or race of people there are some basic questions that are usually asked. What do they call themselves? What language do they speak? How does it differ from mine? What are their religious beliefs? How do they differ from mine? How does their religion influence their culture?

If I apply these questions to myself I arrive at the following answers. I am an American descended from several races. I speak a mixture of midwestern and western American English. My native language was southern jargon. I adopted my present language while attending college and in the work place. I am a Presbyterian Protestant Christian. I mostly follow the Presbyterian beliefs. These are primarily internal beliefs and I do not have to perform any particular actions during the day to demonstrate my religion.

Well now! You know a lot about me if you are a fellow American of similar background. We have a common base of understanding for communication. When I talk about my speech and religion you know and understand what and who I am.

Let's apply these same questions to another group of Americans. They are popularly know as Navajos. Ethnic or Racial purists prefer to call them Native American. This means that they are indigenous to America and never migrated here. While that fits certain religious beliefs, I think you will find, as we pursue the history of these people, that they are immigrants and were still migrating into their present homelands as late as the 1500's.

I call myself an American. Due to certain governmental requirements my race is listed as Anglo or White. My ancestry is a mixture of Irish, Welsh, English and Indian. However, the highest degree of blood comes from my European ancestry. If I wanted to follow the reasoning of others who prefer to be called Native American, I suppose that my correct title would be Non-native American indicating that my ancestors came from somewhere other than America. However it is a little difficult to say I am a Non-native Irish, Welsh, and English American with blood-ties to a Native people or nation. Indian People frequently call their particular group "The People" or "The Human Beings". The earliest reference to Navajos in written documents is thought to have been made by Coronado in 1541, when he referred to them as *"Querechos"* or wanderers. The next reference was as *"Apachu"*. This term was applied by the Spaniard to all of the Athapascan speaking people in the southwest.

In 1626 Father Zarate Salmeron stated that the Jemez Pueblos spoke of a people living north of them between the Chama and San Juan Rivers as *"Apaches de Navaju"*. The term *"Navaju"* roughly translated into planted fields. These people were later referred to in Spanish written materials as *"Apaches de Navaju"*. The term *"Apachu"* was used to mean stranger by the Tewa speaking people at Jemez. So the total name applied to that particular group of people was "Strangers of the Great Planted Field" or something similar.

Later in time the term *"Navaju"* was used separately from *"Apachu"* to distinguish a particular group of people. This group had an exclusive ceremony called the "Blessingway", the basis for all other rituals. They had common linguistic and cultural differences such as weaving, dress, moccasins, hairstyle, and arrows. They resided within an exclusive territory.

These features distinguished them from all others

in the southwest. The term *"Navaju"* received Spanish pronunciation to become *"Navajo"* which has been
accepted as the name for these people through
common usage and written historical usage.[2] The
politically correct name for a person from this group
is a Native American of the Navajo Tribe, one in the
Apachean branch of the Athapascan race.

However, the Navajos may follow the lead of those
residents of southern Arizona who have historically
been called Papagos. They recently amended their
laws, documents and notices to be known by their
real name which is *"Tohono O'odham."* Other Arizona
tribes are seriously considering taking similar action.

The language of the Navajos is a bit more complicated than mine, but is easily described. Most non-
Indians assumed that all Indians were the same,
expecting them to communicate with each other in a
common language. The reasons for this assumption
could possibly come from the following circumstances.

The practice of making war and raiding was
present before the coming of the European. Captives
learned the language of their captors. Since the
trading economy required cross-tribal communication,
many individual Indians learned to speak the language of the tribal group nearest to them geographi-
cally.

European explorers always managed to find Indians who could speak the language that was used by
their neighboring group. It is evident that communication was not always effective. Sometimes three
people were involved in the process of asking and
answering questions. An Indian who could speak
English, French or Spanish and an Indian language
communicated with another Indian who could speak
one of the European languages and the language of
another tribal group who in turn spoke to someone of
the other tribe. The European would refer a question
in his language to the first interpreter who would
then translate to the next person who would translate

and ask the person for whom the question was intended for an answer. When the answer was given,
the process was reversed to relay an answer to the
European. It is little wonder that the communication
between Europeans and Indians was inefficient. One
can imagine the strange impressions that were formed
when questions were asked that had no cultural
reference to the person being asked.

The best way to demonstrate translation difficulties is to use a Navajo tale about a coyote and two
cottontail rabbits. In Illustration 1 the literal English
translation of Navajo is provided as well as the free
English translation. If this is the first step to translation, one can see how adding another language
would increase the difficulties.

CHART 1: EXAMPLE OF TRANSLATION

NAVAJO

Gatbahi|ṃá ii|ndilcháạ'gad
dayiittsá.|Hazhó'ó|ńdadees-
t'ịịgol'inda|Mạ'ii!|Mạ'ii!
daahĭigol|yĭch'ị'|hadadeesh-
ghaazh;|Mạii|bich'ị|chĭ
deeldlo'go|'ańĭ|jinĭ|"Haalá|
'a'hoodzaa,|siкis|yázhĭ|da-
neesкahĭshá|haadaat'é?

LITERAL TRANSLATION

Gray-rabbits|coyote|he-smelling-about
they(dist.pl)saw-him|Carefully|they-
|(dist.pl)having-hidden|then|"Coyote!|
Coyote!|they(dist.pl)saying|they-to-
ward-him|they-(dist.pl)started-to-shout
out.|Coyote|toward-them | he-having-
Smiled|thus-he said|it-is-said,|"What
happened!|my friends|little|they(dist.
pl)are-fat?|how-they(dist.pl)are?.|

FREE TRANSLATION

The cottontails saw coyote sniffing around. After
having hidden themselves carefully, they began shout-
ing at him, saying "Coyote! Coyote!" Coyote, smiling,
said to them, "Well, how do you do? How are my little
fat friends?"[3]

Through centuries of common contact between
speakers of other languages there has been a process
of borrowing and adopting words from German,
French, Italian and Spanish. There are few Athapas-

can words, while other Indian language names and
expressions have been made a part of the American
language. The few Navajo words that have been
picked up are largely used inappropriately or have
an Anglicized pronunciation.

North American Indians speak many languages belonging to distinctly different language families which
do not have a common origin. These languages are
fully developed with highly complex speech forms.
One could equate this difference by comparing English to Hindi.

The language spoken by the Navajo has been
identified as a member of the Nadene language family,
of which there are four: Eyak, Haida, Tlingit and
Athapascan. The Athapascan branch is spoken by
people in the interior of Alaska, Western Canada, the
Northwest Pacific Coast, and the Southwestern United
States. Navajos speak the Athapascan language.
During the last four to five hundred years there has
been a linguistic evolution in the modern forms of the
Athapascan language into Apachean which is spoken
by Navajo, Jicarilla Apache, Chiricahua Apache, and
Lipan Apache tribes in the southwest.[4]

Now it is possible to describe and compare the
language of the Navajos with my language. The
language the Navajos speak is an Apachean dialect of
the Athapascan branch of the Nadene language. I
speak an American dialect of the English branch of
the Indo-European language.

It has been said that a people's language reflects
its culture and beliefs. The Navajo language is called
"dine bizaad" the people's word or language. There
are many differences between the language spoken by
the Navajo and the Old World European languages.

Some of the major differences are included here
for demonstration purposes. There are four basic
vowels-a, e i and o. These vowels are modified by
following distinctive features: (1) long and short

vowels are determined by the length of time used in their production, (2) vowels are either nasalized(said through the nose) or not nasalized, (3) vowels are either high pitched, low, rising or falling in tone, (4) unless vowels are preceded by a consonant, they have a glottal stop before them. This means that a word that sounds and appears the same to a non-Indian can be used for several different meanings by modifying the vowel. For example, possessive pronouns can be changed from "possessive" to "came into possession" (strong emphasis) by changing the vowel from short to long: **"shi"**-my to **"shii"**-possession.[5]

The pronouns are determined by the number of people involved and make no distinction in gender, as demonstrated in the following illustration.

CHART 2:   PERSONAL PRONOUNS

Person Number	Singular (1)	Dual (2)	Distributive (3 or more)
1	shi-I	nihi-we	danihi-we
2	ni-you	nihi-you	danihi-you
3	bi-he,she,it	bi-they	dabi-they
3a	ho-he,she	ho-they	dabi-they

Source: Irvy W. Goosen, *Navajo Made Easier: A Course in Conversational Navajo,*, (Flagstaff: Northland Press, 1968), p.12

Some Navajo words are considered powerful enough to attract good or drive away evil. There are also words that can be very dangerous and are uttered only by special people under very restrictive conditions.

In English, if one dropped a bowl accidentally, one would say, "I dropped the bowl". In Navajo, one would say, "The bowl fell out of my hand". Different verb forms are used in referring to people than are used for animals when they are actors in a statement.

In English, a question is indicated by the way our voice sounds or by a question mark in written materials. The Navajo uses a question indicator that says, "This is a question"."*Sha*" is used instead of words such as what, when, where or who. In short phrases that can be answered with a yes or no,"*Da*" introduces the question. In other instances, it is followed by "*-ish*" which is also a question indicator.

Long numbers are very cumbersome to express in Navajo because of the counting system. A literal translation of $58.99 is "Fifty added to it eight dollars, added to it ninety, and added to it nine cents. The value of coins is denoted by a color, dating back to a time when traders used poker chips or scrip.

Traditionally a Navajo has three names: an English or Spanish name, a name equal to a nickname and a name that only the person and his immediate family knows, which is not used in normal conversation.

Family descent is traced through the mother's clan. Family terms like father, mother, brother, and sister are used in addressing each other within the clan. The father's clan is not nearly as important as the mother's. Relatives are counted through clan membership however distant their actual relationship. A Navajo person is born for the father's clan but is born to his mother's clan.

It is appropriate when introducing one's self to a stranger to say, "I was born for the (name of father's) Clan and born to the (name of mother's) Clan." This enables the stranger to know if they are clan relatives.

A Navajo woman refers to her own and her sister's children by the same title as they are both considered her sons. The Navajo man uses the same title for his son and his brother's children. However, a woman uses the term "*shich'e'e*" for her daughter and the man must use the term "*sitsi'*" for his daughter. The woman calls her son "*shiyaazh*" and the man calls his son *"shiye'"*.

Many of the verbs are so complex that they can only be listed in a paradigm. The paradigm contains all the different forms of the basic verb and its tenses based upon the type of object that is being acted upon or is the actor.[6] If one is to communicate effectively in Navajo, paradigms for verb stems must be memorized.

Navajo is obviously a highly complex, well defined language that expresses all concepts in an oral fashion. There are regional differences in the way that Navajo is spoken. People who live in Canoncito speak differently than those who live at Kayenta. Navajo speakers recognize and understand these differences in much the same way that English speakers recognize a southern or east coast resident.

All people have a story of creation that is extremely significant in their religion. My religion is the Presbyterian branch of Protestantism from the Judeo religion. The events of creation figure prominently in it. In like manner, the Navajo stories of origin are a basis for their religious activities. A more detailed account of these stories can be found in Appendix A.

A ceremony containing events from the Navajo stories of creation is called a "way" which is the path that provides the process to reach a desired goal. The Navajo wishes to attain *"'ił hozhǫ́"*(happiness).

One such "way" is a rite called the Blessingway. This ceremonial is used to provide blessings to a person from the time of birth to old age. These special blessings can only be obtained by participation in this ceremony. The Blessingway provides ceremonies for birth, adolescence, weddings, the home, property, protection against danger, and assistance in prolonging life as long as possible.

Other combinations of events in "ways" are organ-

CHART 3: PARADIGM FOR THE VERB STEM, "HANDLE."

Object	Future	Imperfect	Perfect
Object:One object,anything roundish and hard-bottle,ball	Future	Imperfect 'ą́ą́ł	Perfect 'aah'ą́
Object:Pack, burden, load.	Future yééł	imperfect yeeh	Perfect yį
Object:Plural, separable objects=beans, seeds, money.	Future jih	imperfect jaah	Perfect jaa'
Object:Plural, separable Objects smaller number than above.	Future nil	Imperfect niil	Perfect nil
Object:One animate object baby, cat, sheep.	Future (ł)tééł	Imperfect (ł)teeh	Perfect (ł)tį
Object:Anything on the back baby, load, knapsack.	Future (ł)jił	imperfect (ł)jiid	Perfect (ł)jid
Object:Non-compact matter wool, hay. sand.	Future (ł)joł	Imperfect (ł)jooł	Perfect (ł)jool
Object:Anything in a vessel such as a pail, box, or pan	Future ką́ą́ł	imperfect kaah	Perfect ką́
Object:A slender stiff object=a pole, pencil, broom.	Future tįįł	Imperfect tįįł	Perfect tįįtį
Object:A slender, flexible Object: rope, hair, string	Future lééł	imperfect lé	Perfect lá
Object:Mushy matter mud or plaster.	Future tłoh	imperfect tłeeh	Perfect tłéé
Object:A flexible, flat cloth, sheet, flat paper.	Future (ł)tsos	imperfect (ł)tsóós	Perfect (ł)tsooz

Source: Irvy W. Goosen, *Navajo Made Easier: A Course in Conversa tional Navajo*, (Flagstaff: Northland Press, 1968), p.159

ized according to the needs of the patient.   Some of
the other "ways"   are the Monsterway, Enemyway,
Evilway, and Coyoteway.

The religious reference for Christians is a written
document, the bible, and there are many different
interpretations of it.   The religious reference of the
Navajo is an oral tradition that is passed down
by word of mouth. There are no written procedures
for healers to follow in performing ceremonies for
their patients. One can see why there are
many regional differences in the interpretation and
application of rituals that are learned through memo-
rization only.

Perhaps the best explanation was made by Ethelou
Yazzie when she said:

> "It should be emphasized that
> there are many different versions of
> the origin of the Navajos and of the
> accounts of the various under-
> worlds. Little agreement exists
> regarding the exact number of
> previous worlds or of the events
> which occurred in each: and there
> is a disagreement as to the colors
> assigned to the various worlds.
> Nevertheless,there is a basic accord
> concerning the major events of the
> Tribe's pre-history; and it is said that
> the beauty of the stories of the
> Navajo creation and origin surely
> equals the beauty contained in Gene-
> sis."[7]

There is also disagreement concerning the location
of the four cardinal sacred mountains.   Actually,
there are six mountains that are important to the
Navajos.   There is a mountain at each cardinal point
plus Gobernado Knob and Huerfano Mountain.   The
southern and western mountains are agreed upon by
everyone as being Mount Taylor and the highest of

the San Francisco Peaks, Mount Humphrey.

There is much speculation concerning the exact location of the eastern and northern mountains. One location is near the head waters of the Rio Grande River in the San Juan Mountains near Abiquiu. Abiquiu, Pedernal and Wheeler Peak have been suggested sites. The Jicarilla Apaches who live in New Mexico have identified the mountain of the east as Sierra Blanca Peak in Colorado. There is general acceptance of Hesperus Peak in the La Plata Mountains as the mountain of the north, and Blanca Peak as the mountain of the east, even though it is further north than Hesperus Peak.[8]

Reichard points out that the eastern mountain has been suggested as Blanca or Pedernal Peak. She also points out that for a particular ceremony the Singers went to Wheeler Peak to collect special waters, and upon returning stated that it was too far east.

She explains that Blanca Peak is too far north, and that Wheeler Peak is too far east for the mythical location, which is probably more correctly in the vicinity of Pederanal or Pelado Peaks. Nevertheless, Navajos have used materials from Blanca and Wheeler Peaks for some ceremonies.[9]

The land within the boundaries of the four sacred mountains is the home of the dine. A Holy One was left in each of the sacred mountains. There is one Holy One whose body starts at the foot of Mount Taylor and curves around the outside of the four sacred mountains with the head stopping at Blanca Peak. This Holy One protects the people living inside the boundary. Dine who live beyond the boundary of the four sacred mountains have difficulties with nature for they are out of harmony with the Holy Ones.[10] This boundary is conceptualized in Map 1.

The events of the emergence and post-emergence take for granted that there are other people in the world. However, the Navajo religion attempts to explain only how they themselves came into existence.

   Most Christian religions have a book of common
worship or procedures which point out suggested or
required behavior in everyday as well as formal circumstances.   There is no hierarchy of divinity among
the Holy Ones.   The Navajos have no written form, so
the variants are more common.   Navajo religion is based
upon an origin theory that tries to account for things
in the universe by relating man's activities to it.
Each ceremony uses a special theme with a long description of the activities.   The importance of the theme
is explained during the ceremony by the religious
practitioner, often called Shaman, Medicine Man or
Singer.   It is more appropriate to call him Hatath-
lie(*Hataaɬii*) which means Chanter/ Shaman in Navajo.

   Few things are totally bad or evil and with proper
religious ceremonies, evil can be brought under control.
Once evil is controlled it can either be eliminated or
turned to good.

   The coyote is a central figure in the Navajos'
religious experiences.   He is a symbol or spirit of
slyness and knavery.   He was with First Man and First
Woman in the first world and is in the present world.
He demonstrates the most diverse qualities of mankind.

   The ceremony honoring the coyote was thought to
be extinct, no longer practiced by the Navajos.   There
are many references to this ceremony in Navajo legends
indicating that it was very old.   Karl W. Luckert has
preserved a full nine-day ceremony of the Coyote.   His
work is a vital link to past Navajo practices.   He found
two elderly Hatathlies who could still perform this
healing ceremony.   It was a part of the hunting ceremonies during the time that Navajos depended upon
hunting for survival and incorporated by the Jicarilla
Apaches. It was probably widely used after the Pueblo
Revolt when many Puebloans lived among the Navajos.[11]

MAP 1: THE FOUR SACRED MOUNTAINS

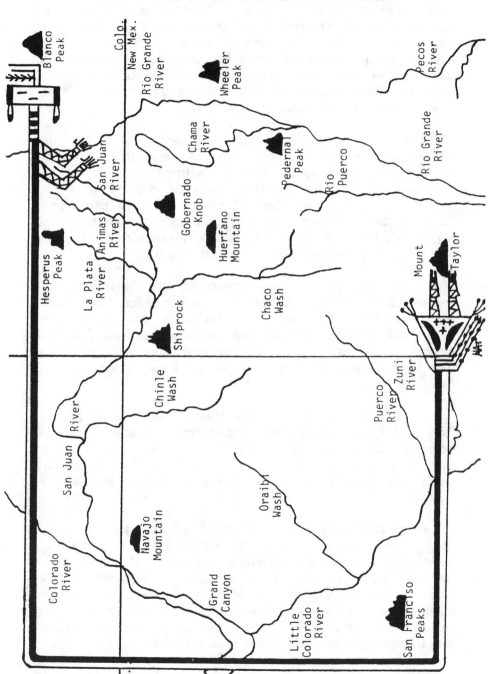

Ceremonies consist of long detailed rituals performed in a required order. The ceremony can last up to nine days and any error or deviation may cause the Hatathlie to start all over at the beginning. The ceremony contains rites for purification, supplication to the Holy Ones, application of symbolical sacred objects, identification of the patient to the gods, and the absorption of good by the patient.

The major use of a religious ceremony is to cure illness and disease. Some illness may be caused by ignoring restrictions of the religion. If a Navajo followed all of the requirements of his religion, he would spend a great deal of time removing the harmful results of broken taboos. Navajos strive to reach an ideal, but, as most of us do, maintain a lifestyle somewhere between the ideal and reality.

If one religious ritual does not cure an illness, a series of rituals are tried until a cure for the illness is discovered. All illness is caused by some error and when this is determined, the person must confess the error. This is a form of bravery, because mythical heroes always confess to mistakes, errors, and failures.

Once the reasons for the illness have been identified and those errors confessed, then the evil can be removed or controlled. Ceremonies are designed to purify as well as to cure. The rituals for attracting good may also be used for the exorcism of evil at the same time.

Purification is a vital part of all religious ceremonies. The use of a sweathouse and emetics are required for most ceremonies. Sexual abstinence, a form of purification, requires the patient to abstain from sexual activity for at least four days before and after the ceremony. Fasting is also a purifying requirement that allows a patient to accept and retain the blessings received from the ceremony.

Wild plants are widely used in the treatment of

illnesses. Some plants are burned and the ashes are used for medicinal purposes. Ethnobotanical studies have identified some 500 species of plants used by Navajo Hatathlies.[12]

The Hatathlie has the choice of many different sandpaintings for any particular ceremony. He selects the most appropriate ones based upon the needs of the patient. When a patient sits on a sandpainting and the Hatathlie treats him with the sacred objects from the medicine bundle and uses the correct chants and prayers, the person becomes as one with a holy person and shares all of the miraculous powers of that particular Holy One.[13]

It is most difficult for the non-Navajo to understand the extremely emotional, religious experiences of an individual in these ceremonies. The patient becomes the focus of all activities for several days during the ceremony and several days following its completion. Friends, relatives and neighbors surround the patient, in support of his well-being, working for his improvement. As a patient undergoes this experience he becomes a holy person in union with the Holy Ones attaining "'i7 hozhǫ",(Happiness).

There is no healing process available to me that includes diagnosis, treatment, psychotherapy, and ceremony all at one time to cure my ills. My medical practitioner has not developed a system that treats the whole person. Illness in my culture is considered a private problem not to be shared with everyone.

The artistic representation of the Holy Ones and their helpers portrayed in sand is valued by many. The process has been duplicated for commercial purposes. A picture is drawn on a piece of pressed wood. Part of the picture is painted with white glue then sprinkled with sand. This is repeated until the board is totally covered and the design is complete. While they are attractive and have the effect of preserving this wonderful art form, the beauty of a fresh sandpainting done in native sand on a buckskin can never be truly reproduced.

Images of the Holy People and their helpers are often copied in the creation of silver jewelry and is woven into Navajo rug designs. These Native American art forms have become widely accepted.

A whole series of animals, insects, snakes, birds, and plants are portrayed in sandpaintings. These characters all play roles in the stories from which the sandpaintings are drawn. The stylized drawings of the bat, great fly, prairie dog, porcupine, rabbit, and bear are beautifully and simply done and are shown in Illustration 1. The bean plant, corn plant, squash and herb plants are also shown in the same beautiful manner as those in Illustration 2.

Hatathlies are paid for their services, a concept arising from the legends of the Navajo. There are many instances in which supernatural beings insisted upon payment for services rendered. For example, the Sun asked for a feather from the headdress of the monster which the twins were to kill, in payment for supplying them with armor and weapons. This concept is accepted as a way of life by Navajos. A person must pay in numerous ways to receive the supernatural benefits of a sing or chant. The Hatathlie is paid in either sheep, blankets, jewelry or cash.

A basic fee is charged for a ceremony. If additional special prayers, sandpaintings or other events are used their costs are added to the basic fee. The Hatathlie may charge a wealthy person a large fee but ask for a much smaller one, for the same service, from a poorer patient. His helpers are paid separately in materials or cash, and are fed during the ceremony.

The highest cost of all may be for food. There is great prestige in having many people at a sing, for many visitors add to the honor and blessings of the patient. If the food is good and plentiful, more people will attend. The cost of meat, flour, baking powder, lard, sugar, vegetables, soda pop, and coffee to feed hundreds of people all day can amount to hundreds of dollars. Usually, relatives and friends assist in the preparation and serving of the food. Families have gone into debt for several years to provide a large ceremony for a loved one or close relative. Those who are poor have a right to call upon family and clan members to help raise the necessary goods and funds for the Hatathlie and the ceremony.[14]

A three day ceremony called a sing or a squaw dance is the most popular ceremony. Those contemplating journeys can be protected by this ceremony while they are outside of the boundaries of the sacred mountains.

People who have been away to war in the armed forces, to school, to work, or just traveling have the ceremony to rid themselves of the evil from outside the sacred area. One can also be held for health reasons. Whatever the reason, each performance of the ceremony will vary according to the individual needs of the patient.

More traditional Navajo people have unique beliefs about death, the avoidance of the dead and burials. The Navajo delays death as long as possible using religious activities to help him stay safe from evil. Yet his life style is not necessarily a safe one. Bravery, even foolhardiness, is admired while cowardice is deplored. When circumstances are beyond his control, the Navajo is usually fatalistic rather than terror stricken and is normally a good loser.

The Navajo does not fear death in the way one might expect. He believes that if a man suffers during his lifetime he has no reason to expect any suffering after death. He tries to control his life through religious ceremonies, but recognizes that he cannot change his ultimate destiny.

ILLUSTRATION 1: SANDPAINTING ANIMALS

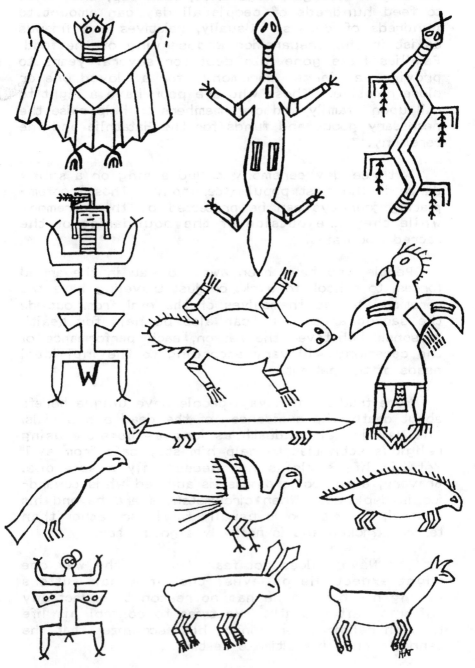

ILLUSTRATION 2:   SANDPAINTING PLANTS

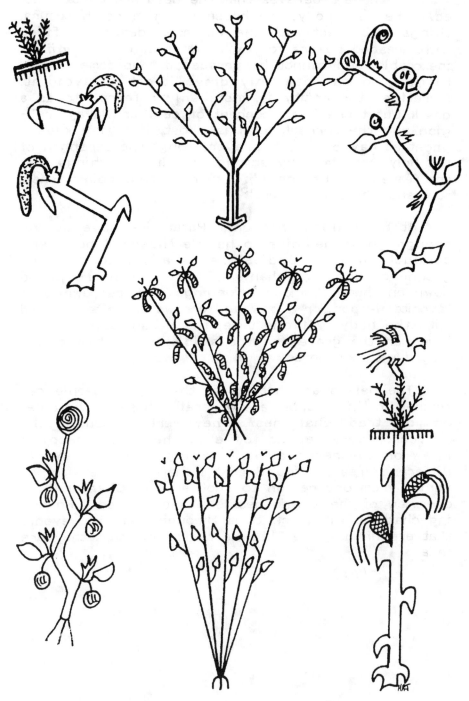

The Navajo believes that the dead are contaminat-
ed. The dead body, the house in which death occurs,
things in contact with the victim at death are filled
with dreaded powers for evil. A ghost or "ch'iidii" is
inexorable, and cannot be persuaded to become helpful
to man, so man can only drive it off or avoid it.
Sometimes the entity is mistakenly referred to as a
devil, but there is no concept of devil in Navajo religion and the correct term is ghost. Man may keep a
ghost at bay by using prayer, song, the strength of
the Holy Ones, and by arming himself with things that
are feared by the "ch'iidii", such as flint points,ashes,
soot and ghost medicines.[15]

It is thought that only Hatathlies have strong
enough ghost medicine to handle the dead body and
conduct burials. Bodies are usually placed in the
ground or under overhangs of cliffs which are pulled
down on them. Various belongings such as jewelry, a
favorite weapon, or a bow and arrows are often buried
with the body. At one time, the person's horse was
killed on the grave and the saddle was mutilated and
placed with the horse.

The beliefs and actions of the Navajo people described in this chapter are generally those of the older
or more traditional ones. They were personally observed or were related to me by the Navajo people I
knew on the reservation. Having lived in several
different areas, I found that beliefs and ceremonies
varied from one region to another. In Chapter I an
overview of the Navajo people was developed. Following chapters will track them through historical events
that explain how they became the people that they are
today.

CHAPTER TWO

THE IMMIGRANTS

Most citizens of the United States can trace their family's migration to their present home. For example one branch of my ancestors migrated directly from Ireland to the United States. They settled in South Carolina. Later the siblings moved to other parts of the country, mainly to Arkansas and Missouri. Another branch found its way to Canada from Ireland and their siblings migrated to Wisconsin and then to Colorado.

The Navajos also migrated to their present site. Drawing conclusions from the available data allows one to describe the following events for these migrants to the southwest.

Most researchers feel that the early Athapascans came over the land bridge of the Bering Straight and then settled into various regions of Alaska and Canada, moving into the Northwestern United States and eventually to the Southwest. No one has pinpointed the exact time frame for this exodus. We don't know why various bands continued to wander, and we can only speculate about the contact they had with other groups and cultures as they followed natural migratory paths.

As the ancestors of the Navajos began filtering into the southwest they found large areas of land bare and deserted. A severe and prolonged drought from 1276 to 1299 caused crop failures, inadequate water supplies and the reduction of game animals. Another prolonged drought occurred from 1573 to 1593. Many Puebloans were forced to leave their original villages to seek more dependable water sources.

Some migrated to western mesas and joined the Hopis. Tree ring dating methods indicate that the Hopi village of Old Oraibi has been continuously inhabited since the late 400 A.D.s. However, due to the limited resources of the area of the Hopi villages, it is doubtful that many immigrants settled there.

Others settled along the Rio Grande, Chama, San Juan, Little Colorado, Puerco Verde, San Francisco, Pecos, Gila and Salt Rivers. Some pueblos were abandoned due to warfare with wandering bands.

The abandoned areas were ideal for the ancestors of the Navajos. They depended upon hunting for food, were learning flood water farming, and lived in small widely scattered bands rather than in villages. Their traditional life style required less water and less productive land than that of the Puebloans.

There are several theories concerning the arrival time of the first Athapascans into the area. The estimates are from around 1000 A.D. to 1500 A.D. Tree ring dating methods identify logs in old hogans from 1300 A.D. to 1598 A.D. It would seem that all of these dates are possible, due to the fact that the early settlers came into the area in small groups and from different directions over a long period of time. It is also probable that some came down the eastern side of the Rocky Mountains into what is now New Mexico along the Rio Grande and San Juan rivers. Since the Pacific Ocean plays a large part in their religious beliefs and ceremonies, others obviously came down the west coast and then inland.

Knowledge about Indian language families is important for comparative linguistics and other scientific approaches in tracing the origins of the American Indian. Glottochronology shows approximately when one language becomes distinct from another. This is calculated by determining the retention of certain test words to develop a percentage of words retained. This percentage helps determine the number of years of separation. By using this method, the following

information becomes available: The Navajos have
been   separated from the Northwestern Coastal Athapascan for 1,000 years, from the Alaskan Athapascan
for 928 years, from the Canadian Athapascan for 628
years, from the Lipan Apache for 355 years, from the
Jicarilla and San Carlos Apache for 279 years, and
from the Chiricahua Apache for 149 years. This linguistic evidence would suggest that ancestors of the
Navajos began their journey from the northern areas
to the southwest as early as 956 A. D.[16]

Mendelian genetics taught that each person inher-
its an equal number of genes from each parent. In
the past 10 to 15 years researchers have identified
structures serving as power sources for the cells
called mitochondria. They are not found among the
46 chromosomes in the cell's nucleus. Sperm cells do
not contain mitochondria DNA. They are passed on
unchanged from mother to daughter providing a
continuous genetic history. Dr. Douglas Wallace,
chairman of genetics and molucular medicine, Emory
University, Atlanta, has led a team in analyzing the
blood cells of Indians in North and South America and
compared them to Asians in Siberia, Eastern Asians,
and the Polynesians on islands in the Pacific Ocean.[17]

Four mitochondrial lineage genes were identified
in Indians and named A,B,C and D. The following was
developed from the data: 1. Combinations of A, C,
and D lineages were found in Asians, Siberians and
Indians such as Ticunas in the Brazilian rain forests,
Mayas in Yucatan, and Pimas in Arizona. 2. Lineage
B only was found in Eastern Asians, Polynesians, and
many Indians, but none in Siberia. 3. Lineage A
only was found in Siberians and Indians of the Na-
Dene group in Alaska, Western Canada, Northwestern
USA and in Southwestern USA.

The genetic coding with the most changes indicate
a more diverse and older population. About 2% to 4%
of the coding mutates every 1 million years or 3 to 6
changes every 10,000 years.   The data from mitochondrial studies is summarized in Appendix E.[18]

Using the data from Appendix E, one can make the following observations: 1.   The Na-dene is one of the newest Indian groups to migrate to the Americas. 2. The migration began in Siberia over the Bering land bridge to Alaska, Northwestern USA and Western Canada.   3.   A second Na-dene migration occurred about 1,000 years ago into the Southwestern USA. These are the present day Navajos and Apaches. This genetic information reinforces the date developed by glottochronology for the immigrations to the southwest by Navajo and Apache ancestors from 956 to 1,000 years ago.

The Navajo can trace his ancestry from Asia to Alaska, from Canada to the southern point of the Rocky Mountains, from the west coast and eventually inland, coming together in northwestern New Mexico and northeastern Arizona.   My ancestors completed their migrations in about 150 years.   The ancestors of the Navajo completed their migrations in 950 to 1000 years.

The southwestern Athapascans retained many of the cultural traits of their northern relatives.   One of these is their elaborate ceremony for a maiden at puberty.   Another is the fear of the dead and all of their possessions.   The traditional structure of the home is typical of the north woods conical frame of poles leaned together and covered with available materials. It is also similar to the igloo snow house with a vestibule at the entrance.   The earliest homes in the southwest were the forked-stick hogans which also had a vestibule entrance.   The southwest moccasin is the same unique design favored by Athapascans. Similar tall clay pots with conical bottoms have been found in northern and southern areas. The system of living in small bands with a common Athapascan language are cultural traits that differ from those of other inhabitants of the southwest. [19]

The pre-European Navajo can be described using the existing data. Though the information cannot be authenticated because of the lack of written documentation, any variations would be minimal.

The land occupied by the Navajos before European contact extended east to the Rio Grande River, north along the San Juan River, south towards the mountains of the Mogollon Rim and west to the mesas of the Hopis and beyond. The largest populations were in the area between the Chama and the Rio Grande Rivers or "Dineta", the "homeland."

There were deep canyons with sheer walls cut into the plateaus and soil ranging in color from black to red or multicolored. There were mountain ranges with forests, volcanic domes and cones, basins, mesas, and large fields of cinders. There was little surface water. Infrequent rains caused flash floods that covered planted fields along the dry washes. The weather was snowy and cold in the winter, hot and dry in the summer, with an adequate season for growing food. The land was not tenable to others but fit the life style of these new migrants perfectly.

The Athapascans had not yet separated into Navajo and Apache. Then at some point in time one group migrated south on the east side of the Rio Grande, settling in the mountains around present day Riodoso, New Mexico and became the Mescalero Apaches. The Blessingway ceremonials and common language unified them as a people.

The family and clan system is reminiscent of the early farm and ranch families of our own pioneer days. Extended family groups lived on large tracts of farm or ranch land which supported them all. These people, like many of my ancestors, shunned city or village living and traveled there only to trade or sell their wares for necessities and then returned to their homes.

The clans were as families and the young people could not marry anyone from the clan, blood relative or not, because it was considered to be incestuous. Many of the traditional Navajo people still feel that way.

The barn dances and lunch box socials of our earlier rural days served the same purpose as the three day ceremonies of these early Athapascans where young ladies chose young men to dance with them under their shawls. We called it ladies' choice.

Because of the scattered rural style of living, there were no chiefs or headmen who controlled all of the tribe. If there was a need to raid for the acquisition of material things, a war leader was selected by the group. The participants could be from one clan or from several and could be either men or women. This person's authority was respected only while on the mission. Upon returning, the leader lost all authority. War leaders were also selected to provide protection from local warfare. Other Indians in the vicinity raided the early Athapascans for food, women and slaves.

All activities were based on a seasonal agricultural calendar. The calendars were particularly important for planting and harvesting. The need for rain had to be a very important concern as well. Each clan selected a person to keep track of the planting seasons so that crops would be planted and harvested successfully. Each clan had a special planting area and they lived near it during the growing season. Once the harvest was over, they usually moved to an area for the winter where there was good hunting. When there were droughts, imaginative leaders mounted forays against the Pueblos where crops, irrigated by water from the rivers, were plentiful.

Seeds were gathered in season from the yucca, saltbrush, pinon and prickly pear along with wild berries. Corn was dehydrated in heated earthen pits and stored for winter use, when it would be rejuvenated in boiling water as needed. Dried corn was also stored for later use, to be ground into meal for bread. Meat was dried or jerked to preserve it. Food was kept in pottery jars sealed with adobe and stored in small caves and underground pits.

While the crops grew and after the harvest, hunting supplemented their diet.   Hunting activities included snaring small animals such as the cottontail rabbit, pocket gopher, white throated rat, beaver, rock squirrel, silky pocket mouse, deer mouse, meadow vole, spotted skunk, weasel, gray fox, jack-rabbit, porcupine, prairie dog, and a variety of birds. They ate deer and elk. Some buffalo were killed, but they were not found in the general vicinity.

Hunters erected walls of piled brush several feet high in two converging wings leading to a circular trap that was 50 yards in diameter. Antelope were herded into this area and slaughtered.   The antelope hunts must have fostered a festive occasion when they were successful. One can imagine the older men, women and children noisily driving the antelope toward the retaining walls and then into the circular trap.   The hunters were hidden with their weapons waiting for the animals Many animals were killed as they milled around the circle looking for an exit.

Once the killing was done, the work of skinning the animals began and the usable body parts were prepared for cooking or drying. No doubt there were great feasts for everyone. Religious ceremonies were performed to honor the dead animals. Some of the meat was eaten immediately, most of it was jerked or dried in the sun.   The hides, antlers and bones were prepared for transportation to the home area.

When the snows fell and the land became cold, skins were tanned and used for clothing or other utility items. Buffalo and deer skins were tanned with the hair on them and used as robes and bed-ding. Weapons were manufactured. Winter religious ceremonies were performed.   Beads were made from bone, turquoise and shell, and strands of these beads were made to be worn around the neck and in the ears. Leather bow guards were made for the arms. Fasteners were made of bone or shell in the form of buttons and pins. All of these tasks were difficult and time consuming. There was never time just to sit and be idle.

Fields were small due to the lack of plows and draft animals. The basic farming implements were digging sticks and wooden hoes. Special care was used in spring planting. In flood irrigation farming, location and timing were essential. Seeds had to be planted deeply enough so they would not blow away with the spring winds, and yet be in contact with moisture seeping below the surface. The seeds must be planted high enough from the center of the flood plain so the water would not wash them out of the ground when the rains came.

As families grew, they built forked-stick homes, round homes, leantos and rock storage shelters. They also had outside fire hearths, metate rests, undercut pits and meat drying racks.

Wild plants were gathered and used for medicinal purposes. Some plant products were used to poison arrows for hunting and for warfare. Certain plants were chewed much like tobacco while others were used for cleansing and purifying the body during religious ceremonies.

The relationship of the Navajo to the other sur-rounding tribes was one of intermittent peace and raiding. The Athapascan group was relatively small in number. The largest single group of Puebloans at that time was probably the Hopis. Puebloans were numerous along the Rio Grande River but lived in smaller villages. Map 2 shows the pre-European loca-tion of villages.   The Utes lived in the north, the Hualapais, Yavapais and Havasupis in the west.

These early Athapascans were a patriarchal socie-ty. Later cultural changes established a matriarchal society, probably through Puebloan influences. The life of the early Navajo was not an ideal one, for there were many hardships. They were dependent upon the weather for crops to see them through the winter, the availability of game was a major factor, and health problems were largely incurable. Death from dental problems, wounds and injuries is abundantly evident in the bone remains of these early people.

The early Navajo habitat was also limited by the available water. Water was transported in cured animal stomach linings, gourds and woven baskets treated with pinon pine tree pitch.

Remarkable interaction and development was accomplished without benefit of either riding or draft animals. The people walked or ran everywhere and acted as draft animals carrying their belongings, food and water. Moving to the planting fields in the spring and back to the winter home in the fall were major undertakings.

There were trading missions to the Pueblos to exchange deer skins, meat, animal fat, weapons and other items for corn, beans, squash, woven cotton materials, and pottery. When a clan visited the Pueblos for trading it must have been similar to the African safaris of later years. Everything was carried from one place to another on foot.

One wonders how a raiding party escaped pursuers while carrying the booty on their backs. The ability to run long distances had to have been a highly desirable skill.

It is understandable that the migrations were slow because everyone walked the thousands of miles involved in this period of expansion. What drove them those hundreds of years to move on to other areas? There were, no doubt, territorial conflicts as the populations increased in size, overcrowding the area in which they lived, or whenever a band or group moved into an area already being used by others.

MAP 2: PRE-EUROPEAN PUEBLO SETTLEMENTS

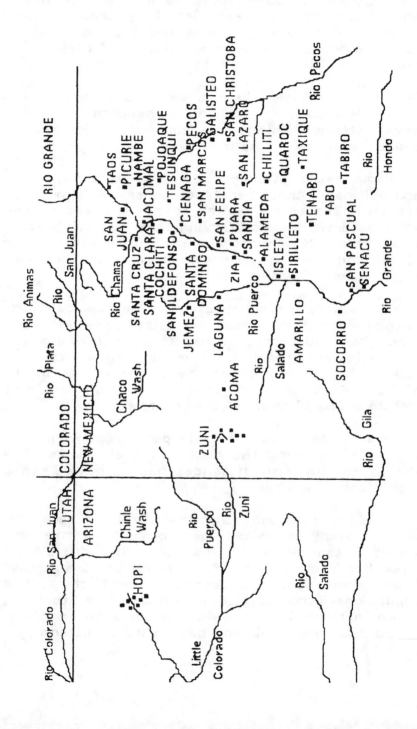

Previous assumptions are reinforced by this early description of the Navajos by Father Alonso de Benavides. He described them in the following Manner:

> "They are very vigorous and warlike people and very brave in war; even in a manner of speaking they stand apart from the other nations; because they speak quietly and slowly, and it seems that the Apaches break their heads in speech. They do not live in villages nor in houses but in tents and clustered camps (rancherias) because they move from mountain range to mountain range looking for game on which to live, although each camp group has a recognized area of land on which they plant corn and other seeds.
>
> They dress in buckskin made of deer hides, very nicely tanned and elegant in their style; and the women are smartly and modestly dressed.
>
> They practice no idolatry other than that of the sun, and even that is not general among them. They laugh at other nations that have idols. It is their custom to have as many wives as they can support, and on the one they catch in adultery, which is unpardonable, they cut off her ears and nose and then divorce her.
>
> They are very obedient to their elders for whom they show great respect; they teach and punish their children, unlike the other nations, who use no punishment whatsoever; and they take great pride in speaking the truth; holding in

dishonor anyone caught in a lie.
And although being one nation they
all speak the same language, the
nation is so extensive that minor
variations are not lacking in some
groups; but they are not such
that cannot be very well
understood.[20]

CHAPTER THREE

THE SPANIARDS

The early migration to and the development of the Athapascans in the southwest was interrupted by another migration that began further to the south. It was to have a major impact upon their lives and culture.

It is almost impossible to imagine two more diverse cultures than the Athapascan and the Spanish. A space ship full of aliens landing in Chicago would be roughly equivalent to the impact of the Spaniard on the Indians of the Americas.

The Spaniards who came to the Americas were adventurers looking for personal wealth and fame through pillage and conquest. Many were refugees from the religious abuses of the Inquisition perpetrated by the Church in Spain. Others were criminals and mercenaries hired to follow their leaders, as well as female camp followers and other support people for the Conquistadors.

The Spaniards ascribed to the ancient concept of civilized and barbaric peoples. Unfortunately there are those who still support this philosophy. The Spaniards automatically assumed that all Indian groups and tribes were heathen barbarians as opposed to the Spanish way of life which had a Christian and civilized quality superior to that of any barbaric Indian.

The obligation of the priesthood and civil authorities was to civilize the barbarians by converting them to Christianity. The next step was to build decent homes and to provide appropriate dress. The Span-

iards would provide towns and a form of government
consistent with a civilized people.

It was obvious to the Spanish officials that the
Indians worshipped pagan idols and that their religion represented the devil.   Indians did not control
their personal affairs, their sexual lives or their civil
affairs.   They dressed indecently and their houses
were not fit for human beings.

They further reasoned that the Indians should be
most grateful to receive Christianity, an organized
government and an advanced form of society. Indians
were not to have a voice in the form of government
or the religion being imposed upon them, for it was
deemed a sufficient reward to live with such refine-
ment.[21]

Priests, civil authorities and the military neither
understood nor cared that these people had an old
and advanced culture that was adapted to the particular area where they lived.   Consequently an opportunity for the residents to progress under intelligent
and humane guidance was never provided.

The documented history of this period was written by the Spanish and expressed their point of view.
It is reasonable to assume that the early Navajos
were frequent visitors to the pueblos of the Rio
Grande area and participated in the widespread
system of bartering.   The fact that the Spaniards
made very few references to them in the early
records indicates that the Navajos knew about the
Spaniards before the Spaniards knew about the
Navajos.

The Spanish exploration of the southwest began
soon after   Cabeza de Vaca returned to northern
Mexico from a shipwreck on the Texas coast in 1535,
carrying rumors of rich cities in the north. The
speculation about fabled cities of gold have been a
part of the legend of the southwest ever since that

time.   The pueblos along the Rio Grande River must
have been the "fabled cities" to the people of northern Mexico and the surrounding area.

These pueblos were well established trade centers
and their goods and crafts were desired by others
far and near.   When the villages were described,
through the cumbersome process of interpretation, the
Spaniards felt that they had found another source of
wealth like that of the Aztecs in Mexico.   They had no
reason not to believe that there were more golden
cities in the north just waiting to be plundered.

Officials authorized Fray Marcos de Niza, a missionary, to travel north to find these fabled cities in
1539.   Esteban, a black slave of Cabeza de Vaca who
spoke several Indian languages, accompanied the mission.   The Fray sent Esteban ahead of the group to
prepare a welcome as they approached the villages of
the Zuni.   However, Esteban violated some Zuni taboo
and he was killed. When Fray de Niza heard about
Eteban's death he speedily returned to Mexico without
actually seeing any of the Zuni villages.

Francisco Vasquez de Coronado left Culiacan,
Mexico in April of 1540 with a group of men to look
for the cities of gold, using   the information provided by Fray Marco de Niza.   They followed the same
trails used by Esteban to the villages of the Zuni.

When the group reached the first village of
Hawikuh they found it was deserted.   But as they
proceeded north, they encountered the Zunis who
attacked in force.   Coronado defeated the Indians and
moved into the main villages to sack them.   The
disappointment must have been great when no gold or
silver was found..

The soldiers became angry and threatened Fray
de Niza for lying to them about riches and he fled
back to Mexico. Coronado decided that these were the
wrong villages and that he would continue the search.

The Indian interpreters told Coronado of the Hopi villages to the west. Pedro de Tovar and Fray Juan de Padilla were sent to the Hopi villages, but again they were disappointed to find that there was no gold or silver. Lopez de Cardena journeyed farther west and discovered the Grand Canyon, but no villages of gold.

Hernando de Alvarado was sent east to the villages along the Rio Grande River valley. He passed the village of Acoma but avoided it because of its excellent fortification on a high mesa. He commandeered a village in the Rio Grande Valley for his headquarters and sent word back to Coronado who then moved to this new village.

Coronado's troops lived on the food taken from the Puebloans. Whenever the Indians objected they were easily overridden by the troops with their horses and weapons. Several villages were abandoned by their occupants who went to live with surrounding tribes.

Coronado and 30 of his men began a search for the fabled cities of Cibola in eastern New Mexico, Texas, Oklahoma and a part of Kansas. They traveled north and east as far as the Arkansas River and beyond into Colorado. The searchers returned home without finding any cities and the conflict between explorers and natives was renewed. Coronado was disheartened by his failure to find wealth. There was no gold or silver, only pottery, animal skins, cotton fabrics and vegetables. When the soldiers appropriated these items, the Indians fought back.

Coronado returned to Mexico during April in 1542, empty handed, exactly two years after embarking on his search. He left three missionaries, several Mexican Indians, and a few black slaves in the villages. He must have felt that conditions would be better for them after the soldiers left and that they would be safe. He was gravely mistaken. Frays Padilla and Cruz were killed on a trip to the east looking for a legendary city called "Quievira". Servants brought this information back to Mexico when they returned after the priests were killed. The fate of the third priest, Fray Luis is unknown.

Coronado had provided the Indians of the area with their first impressions of the Spaniards. He had not come to settle the land, but to take its reported wealth of gold. He assured himself a place in history by his great efforts in exploring thousands of miles of unmapped land while searching for the fabled "Cities of Gold". But without horses, Coronado could never have explored such vast areas.

The Indians were awe stricken by the horses used by Coronado's troops. The advantages for transportation and warfare were quickly recognized by all concerned, so when the horse came, it was immediately accepted and gladly acquired by the Athapascans.

The first documented Indian horsemen were found in northern Mexico, and from there the horse spread quickly into present day Arizona and New Mexico. The Spaniards kept the Puebloans under their control on foot, but their free cousins became mobile very quickly. As the Spaniards raided the tribes of northern Mexico for slave labor to work in the mines of Mexico, warfare raged throughout the region. This situation was a further cause for the rapid spread of the horse. By 1580 horses were owned by Indians in northern Mexico and southern Arizona. By 1620 large herds of wild horses roamed the northern regions of Mexico.[22]

After Coronado returned to Mexico, the Rio Grande valley was quiet for almost 40 years. Gaspar Castano de Sosa left Mexico in 1651 with settlers, servants, livestock and wagons loaded with supplies, in the first attempt to colonize the Rio Grande valley. Sosa's group traveled up the Pecos River to the future site of Fort Sumner. They turned west and captured Pecos Pueblo. They continued on to the Rio Grande valley and found several deserted villages. But since

Sosa had not received royal authorization for his venture, Captain Juan Marlete was sent to bring the group back to Mexico.[23]

In 1582 Antonio de Espejo and Fray Bernalidino Beltran led an expedition to look for wealth. The band of explorers followed the Rio Grande River to Zia Pueblo which had been evacuated in advance of their party. They turned east and traveled past Acoma and on to Zuni. Part of the army wanted to return to Mexico while others wanted to visit the Hopi Villages. Espejo took 150 Zuni warriors with him to the land of Tusayan(Hopi) where they visited Awatobi, and then traveled on to the Little Colorado River looking for possible mining sites in the area. They journeyed south to Mormon Lake, into Oak Creek Canyon and on to the Verde Valley, where they found a large deserted pueblo, probably the ruins now called Montezuma's Castle or Tuzigoot ruins.

The explorers met Yavapais and Apaches who were living near the present site of Jerome. Copper traces were found nearby, but no gold or silver. The disappointed Espejo returned through the Hopi Villages to Zuni.

As Espejo's men traveled east from Zuni, they burned fields and houses at Acomita and fought off the local people as well as other Indians who came in to help the locals. These were probably early Navajos and this was their first recorded conflict with the Spaniards. The eastward trek then led to Puaray Pueblo, where Espejo ordered the execution of thirty Puebloan men in revenge for the deaths of the three missionaries left by Coronado. Espejo continued traveling east to the Pecos River and turned south to Mexico without further incident.

Captain Francisco Lyva de Bonilla led the next group of soldiers on an expedition and commandeered San Ildefonso Pueblo for his headquarters. The troops harassed the Puebloans for almost a year. He, as those before him, traveled east on the Great Plains to look for Quievira. The expedition ran short of food and the constant attacks by local Indians caused low moral among the troops. Gutierrez de Human killed Bonilla and assumed command. He marched north to the Kansas River where the Wichita Indians set fire to the grass around the Spaniards and killed the soldiers. Their Indian servants were allowed to return to Mexico where they reported the fate of the expedition.

The first royal order for the settlement of New Mexico was issued to Juan de Orate in 1598. Orate moved rapidly into his new province. He captured the Pueblo at Socorro, made visits to the Santa Domingo, Picuris, Taos, San Xupal, Gallistro, Pecos and Jemez Pueblos. He selected the San Juan pueblo for his headquarters, and from there he visited Acoma, Zuni and the Hopi villages. Captain Marcos de los Godos traveled over the same route from the Hopi lands that Espejo had taken. He brought back samples of copper ore from the Verde Valley area.

Juan de Valdivar left San Juan Pueblo to join Orate in the west. At Acoma he demanded supplies and a battle erupted during which Valdivar was killed. The survivors reported his death and Orate decided to make an example of Acoma for taking the life of a Spanish Officer. He attacked the pueblo in force, slaying more than 800 men, women and children. He marched the surviving 500 women and children and 80 men to San Juan. The males 25 years of age and older had one foot cut off and were sentenced to 20 years of servitude. Men from 12 to 25 years old were sentenced to 25 years of servitude. Women over 12 were sentenced to 25 years of servitude. Girls under 12 were given to Fray Alonso Martinez to distribute to whom he pleased. The boys under 12 were given to Vicentes de Valdivar, the brother of Juan de Valdivar. The remaining survivors were turned out of the village to perish, but were befriended by Indians in the vicinity. Most of the enslaved people were eventually freed by Indian raiders and returned to their homeland.[24]

Valdiver continued his conquest by destroying three Joman Tampiro pueblos, killing many of the inhabitants. Four hundred men, women and children were enslaved and each soldier was rewarded with one slave. These acts of cruelty caused wide spread hostility. By 1600 the conflict was so heated that supplies and materials had to be brought to Oñate from Mexico.[25]

Oñate's lust for gold led him over the same trails to the east looking for the rumored city of riches, Quievira. He returned in 150 days and found several abandoned villages and only one priest with 25 Indians at San Gabriel.

The Navajos welcomed the Puebloans from the villages who brought Spanish trade goods and livestock with them as well as their weaving and pottery skills. The Navajos were evidently not worthy of notice by the Spaniards because they lived in small mobile bands.

The Puebloans were captives of their life style, living in pueblos or villages which fit in with the Spanish method of conquest. Indians greatly outnumbered the Spaniards but the tribes acted independently of each other. Old animosities, predating the Spaniards, could not be settled. Trading provided the major contact between tribes. Meat, robes and fat were traded for cotton blankets, pottery and maize. A tribe did not retaliate against the Spaniards unless their members were directly affected.

Oñate taxed each household one cotton blanket or tanned deerskin annually and maize monthly. A large part of the economy for the Puebloans was the ability to trade with other Indians. When the Spaniards began taxing their trade goods for themselves, it jeopardized the whole system of bartering.

By the end of the 1500's the Spaniards were firmly entrenched in the Rio Grande Valley and the period of occupation and settlement had begun. Oñate

was unsuccessful in his attempt to find gold in the
east so he made one final attempt to find it in the
west. In the fall of 1604, he took 30 men and traveled
through the Hopi Villages to the Colorado River in the
west. He followed it to the Gulf of California. When
Oñate failed to find gold he returned to the valley of
the Rio Grande.[26]

The Indians tribes surrounding the Pueblos were
using horses in the early 1600's. In their written
reports, the Spaniards expressed a deep concern
about this development on the frontier. The early
Navajo were among those Indian horsemen.

The King of Spain removed Oñate from office in 1606
and appointed Pedro de Peralta to replace him. Oñate
resigned in 1607 but it took Peralta until 1609 to
arrive on the scene.

The Spanish governmental concept of towns was
established in Mexico and further south, but this was
never considered as a possibility for the Indian
residents in the Rio Grande area. The villages supported the missionaries and others Spaniards because
the new settlers could not produce sufficient food or
other necessities to sustain themselves. The cost of
constant warfare with other Indians made it impera-
tive to take produce, manufactured goods and enforced labor from the villages. There were many
villages along the Rio Grande River with thousands of
inhabitants who became captives in their own villages
in order to support the Spaniards.

Peralta constructed the first Spanish settlement in
the Rio Grande Valley. It was named San Gabriel del
Yumque and was located between the Chama and Rio
Grande Rivers. It was isolated from the Pueblos and,
consequently, was repeatedly attacked by the Indians
in that area. The settlement had to be abandoned and
the people moved back to more populated areas. The
abandoned settlement was located in an area inhabited
by the Athapascans who later became known as Jicarilla Apaches.

Peralta established Sante Fe as the capital of New Mexico in 1610. Since that date, it has been a capital for three different governments and one state, continuously, for over three hundred and eighty years.[27] This fact is overlooked by most historians when they draw time lines for the United States.

The Franciscan Missionaries decided that they needed the villages for missionary sites. They planned to use the people and their products to support the church. When mission communities were established, people were disciplined for not attending church and corporal punishment was used to make them work in the fields. Whipping posts and stocks were common and public punishment was routine. The extreme harshness of the missionaries eventually caused rebellion in some pueblos.

Civil authorities also needed to maintain their economy. Both factions increased their efforts to create conflict between the Puebloans and the other tribes so the Pueblos would be forced to help provide protection. This bitter conflict continued for the next 34 years.

The military, controlled by the Governor, reduced its protection of the missionaries so much that the Hopi, Zuni, Jemez and Taos Pueblos were able to kill their priests without fear of reprisal.

The governor increased the tax to one yard of cloth, two and one half bushels of maize and personal services for family members each year.

Luis de Rosas became governor in the 1630s and continued the effort to control the missionaries. He raided Pecos Pueblo for slaves and arrested the resident priest, returning him to Sante Fe. He allowed the Indians to rustle livestock from the mission herds. The church followers, in turn, raided the governor's herds and those of his followers.

Rosas removed the priests from Nombre, San Ildefonso, and Santa Clara Pueblos.   The only mission remaining by 1640 was in the Santo Domingo Pueblo.

The Franciscan faction killed Rosas and installed Flores, one of their followers, as governor, but in 1642 the crown appointed Alonzo Pacheco de Heriedia as the governor of New Mexico.   Heriedia established harsh controls over the Pueblos and increased the tax levy to one cotton blanket and two and one half bushels of maize per household every four months instead of annually.

In Spain the Church and Crown finally negotiated an agreement in 1644, and Fernando de Arguello was appointed to replace Heriedia as governor.   Arguello established peace between the Franciscans and the civil authorities.[28]

CHAPTER FOUR

REBELLION AND CHANGE

The Spaniards now turned their attention to the Navajos. Military campaigns were for the sole purpose of obtaining slaves and livestock. Hostility between the Navajos and the Puebloans increased when the Navajos rescued members of their tribe and replaced livestock. The Navajos attacked the Zuni Pueblo of Hawikuh and killed Zunis and the priest.

The Spaniards launched a major campaign deep into Navajo territory in 1678 bringing back goods, livestock and many Navajos as slaves. While the Spaniards and Navajos were locked in warfare, the Puebloans had time to plan a rebellion. The scheme to remove the Spaniards quickly passed from tribe to tribe. Navajo leaders eagerly agreed to participate in the venture and in 1680, combined Indian groups killed 380 Spaniards and 21 priests at Taos and Picuris Pueblos.

Sante Fe fell to the Indian forces on August 13th and the Spaniards retreated down the Rio Grande River. Oterim and 2,000 survivors arrived at El Paso. A counter attack force of 146 Spaniards and 112 Indians went north to recapture New Mexico. In December, 1681, they sacked Isleta and burned the kivas. In quick succession San Felipe, Santo Domingo, Cochiti, Sandia, Alemeda and Puaray Pueblos were retaken. But the united Indians defeated the Spaniards in January, forcing them to retreat again. The Spaniards destroyed Isleta and carried 400 villagers off to El Paso as slaves.[29]

The rebellion was one of the few times that the tribes acted in concert with one another. The history of this country would undoubtedly have been different had there been cooperative warfare among the Indians. On two other occasions they did join together briefly, once in New Mexico and years later at the Little Big Horn, and they were invincible. Great celebrations were held after the Spaniards were defeated. The old religious ceremonies were installed again and practiced without fear of reprisal. The goods left by the Spaniards as they retreated were highly valued as trading items. Then Utes and Comanches began to increase their raiding practices against the Puebloans and Navajos to gain their share of the wealth.

The horse gave the Indians great mobility and speed, allowing them to expand their trading and living areas. Domesticated livestock provided food without depending on hunting.

The old enmities soon resurfaced, kindling suspicions and encouraging warfare, providing an opportunity for the return of the Spaniards. Diego de Vargas, appointed governor of New Mexico, and his army, reached the first Pueblos by 1693. He found them deserted, the people gone. The Keres of Pecos and Cienequilla knew that they would receive no help from the other tribes and decided on a policy of appeasement with the invaders.

Vargas established a temporary headquarters at Bernallio and then proceeded to Santa Ana, Zia and Jemez. On December 16, 1693, he entered Sante Fe. The men had fled so he took the women and children as slaves. After reestablishing the capital in Sante Fe, Vargas captured the tribes one by one. In April he sacked the peaceful Keres Pueblo of Cienequilla, killing the men and taking another 300 women and children as slaves. In July, Jemez was sacked and, by September, Acoma, Zuni and Hopi Pueblos were the only ones remaining free. The great Indian rebellion had ended and once again the Rio Grande Valley belonged to the Spaniards.[30]

The Navajos began to attack the Zuni and Hopi Pueblos and when the villagers complained, Vargas asked them to move to the Rio Grande Valley so that he could protect them from the Navajos. His request was quickly rejected.

In 1696 the Puebloans tried another revolt without help from the other tribes and an estimated 2,000 Indians perished in the snow fleeing from the Spaniards. After this defeat many Puebloans abandoned their villages and went to live with other Indians, primarily the Navajos.

The population of the Navajos doubled during the next fifty years as more and more Puebloans escaped from the harsh conditions imposed by the Spaniards. Pottery shards indicate that Puebloans from almost every village went to live with the Navajos at that time. The Puebloans built cut-stone square houses among the traditional round hogans of the Navajos on isolated high mesas. They also built two and three story stone watch tower/forts for protection against the Utes and Comanches. These forts were not unlike those built in Europe. They served as watch towers, living areas, and fortresses when attacked by enemies.

The Navajos learned to use stones to build their round houses from the Puebloans. This was an excellent substitute for logs in areas where trees were scarce. They also learned to use short logs to build a domed, or cribbed roof.[31]

The Puebloans brought their livestock and material goods garnered from the Spaniards. Surely, the Navajos were delighted with these additions. The Puebloans also brought the art of weaving, traditionally a male skill, which was quickly picked up by the Navajo women. Navajo men did not learn to weave but hunted, farmed and raided as needed. The Navajo women maintained their traditional dress style. They preferred a loose dress made from two blankets fastened at the shoulders and at the waist so that

they could cook around a fire, or ride a horse with
ease.   The Puebloan women preferred their single
piece, close fitting dress.

   The Navajos expanded their cultural beliefs to
include   the origin myth, the importance of descent
from the matrilinial clans, and the matrilocal hogan.
They maintained original Athapascan traits such as
the belief in the Hand-Trembler and Star-Gazer for
diagnosing illness, and those healers who suck foreign objects from patients.   They also kept the
Hatathlie's part of the religious system for healing.

   Puebloans mated with Navajos and never returned
to the Pueblos or their people.   The Navajos have
always had the ability to accept and employ useful
new things from other cultures. They readily adopted
weaving, livestock raising, building techniques, farming methods, and some religious ceremonies from the
Puebloans while retaining their own unique language
and culture.[32]

   These great and rapid cultural changes would
never have occurred if the Spaniards had not caused
the Puebloans to migrate to the Navajos.   The Navajos immediately embraced most of the skills and material goods of the Spaniards plus the substantial
crafts and knowledge of the Puebloans.

   The Navajos no longer had to depend on hunting
to survive.   They were no longer wanderers but
maintained their cherished way of living in small
bands in the isolated valleys and mesas of their new
lands.   The horse allowed them to expand this territory significantly.

   This material wealth also aroused the envy of the
Utes, Comanches, and Spaniards.   The Spaniards increased their purchase of slaves from Indian tribes
causing intertribal wars to intensify.   Tribe plundered tribe for slaves to sell to the Spaniards.

ILLUSTRATION 3:   PUEBLO STYLE INFLUENCE ON
THE NAVAJO HOME

The Round Stone House

The Cribbed Log House

The Spaniards brought horses, cattle, donkeys, mules, sheep, goats, wheat and watermelons from Spain. They also brought metal utensils, metalworking techniques and finely woven materials. Weaving from wool rather than native cotton became popular with the Indians immediately.[33] In turn, the Indians introduced the Spaniards to chili, corn, indigo plants, and their earthen ovens.

The struggle for domination in the Rio Grande Valley and surrounding areas in the 1600s was unusual and bloody. The long struggle between the church and the civil authorities was costly to the Indians--the rebellion was a natural action for survival-- but by 1700 the area was firmly under the control of the Spaniards.

At the turn of the century, the Navajos were described as being 100 leagues from north to south, to the boundaries of the Utes and Comanches and on the west to the valleys of the Little Colorado River. Another description places them thirty leagues west of Jemez, from there to the San Juan River and east to a point of forty leagues then west to Chama. The first description was probably the more accurate one.[34]

In order to keep the Indians from attacking them, the Spaniards deemed it necessary to keep the various tribes hostile towards each other. Slavery was sanctioned so that tribal strength would be weakened and governmental officials would benefit financially at the same time. The Spaniards coerced the Apaches into raiding the Comanches; the Utes raided the Navajos, and the Navajos raided the Pawnees and Witchitas of the plains. The Spaniards were eager to buy Indian slaves from any group that offered them.

The 1700s were a bloody period of time. The land was settled along the Rio Grande River and the Spaniards wanted to expand. They used the warfare between tribes to better their lives, but it did strain their resources. The following events are illustrative of the turmoil of the time.

The Hopis destroyed Awatobi at the turn of the century, killing the men and the priests because the Pueblo had allowed the priests to return. All of the women and children were taken into other villages. Awatobi lies in ruins to this very day.

From 1720 to about 1760 there were few conflicts between the Navajos and the Spaniards. Instead, the Spaniards encouraged the Utes and the Comanches to carry out warfare against the Navajos. The Navajos living nearest the Spaniards allowed the priests to come back among them at Encinal and Cebolleta so they would have protection from the warring tribes. The Navajos moved west to Canyon de Chelly, abandoning the older homes in the northwest part of New Mexico. In 1750 the Navajos drove out the priests and warfare with the Spaniards increased.

Land grants were issued in the Mount Taylor, Encinal, and Rio Puerco River areas in the 1760s. The Navajos and the Gila Apaches drove the settlers from the land grants and raided Laguna, Zia, Santa Clara, Jemez, San Ildefonso, Abiqui, and Albuquerque. This caused Governor Mendinueta to encourage the Utes and Comanches to raid the Navajos for slaves.[35]

As the Navajos were forced west they came into conflict with the Hopis, Yavapais, and Havasupais. During the 1780s the Navajos killed or carried off most of the Hopis. The population decreased from 8,000 Hopis in 1775 to approximately 800 by 1780, with only a few villages occupied.

Dominquez and Escalante began their explorations in 1776 and marched completely around the perimeter of the Navajo lands. They crossed the San Juan River to the north and traveled over large areas of what is now Colorado, Utah and Arizona before returning to New Mexico. This amazing feat is a story in itself.

One of the most effective Spanish governors of

New Mexico was Governor Juan Bautista de Anza. His
qualifications included an excellent concept of the
frontier situation and the Indian conflicts. He was
also a superior tactician. Soon after becoming governor, de Anza decided that the alliance between the
Gila Apaches and the Navajos must be broken. He
forbade the Navajos to visit the Puebloans to trade.
Instead, he sent Spanish traders among the Navajos
in their own lands to peddle Spanish wares. In 1786
he collaborated with the headmen from San Mateo,
Cebolleta, Chuska Mountain, Ojo del Oso, and Canyon
de Chelley to break with the Gila Apaches. This
alliance lasted as long as he was governor.

The French were expanding into the plains areas
with their trading centers. They now had posts on
the Missouri, Platte, and Arkansas Rivers and in
Texas. They supplied the Pawnee, Comanche, Kiowa
and other tribes with weapons, powder and shot. The
tribes could sell any plunder from New Mexico
through these trade centers. The Comanches attacked
Albuquerque in 1774 to get goods for trade.[36]

Governor de Anza knew that if the armed Indian
tribes continued raiding, it would be the end of the
Rio Grande settlements. He expanded the itinerant
trading system to include not only the Navajo and
Apache lands, but also into the plains, where Spanish
wares were peddled to all tribes. This gave the
Spaniards a market for the goods from the Rio Grande
Valley but tied them to the plains Indians. These
itinerant traders who roamed the prairies of the
southwest, trading with all Indian tribes, became
known as "Comancheros".[37]

The most profitable economy was still slavery.
Trade Fairs were established for this purpose by the
authorities for the residents of the Rio Grande Valley.
The brutality of these trade fairs was described as
being as harsh as any of the Roman or Near Eastern
slave markets. Not only Spanish slavers brought
captives, but Indians brought other Indians to sell.
Captives young enough to accept training by the

Spaniards were the most valuable commodity. Church records in New Mexico are full of baptismal records of Indians who were chattel of the Spaniards.[38]

A form of Navajo economy developed during this period, based upon the ownership of goods and people. A class system consisting of wealthy Navajos who had large flocks of livestock, slaves and goods and the poorer Navajos who tended the herds and depended upon others for their livelihood. For the poor, the only route to wealth was the system of raiding. If a raiding party was successful, the members became wealthy overnight.

It was only natural that when talk of war came up, the "Ricos" or wealthy owners preferred peace. They did not want to risk reprisal raids by the Spaniards and other tribes. The poorer members wanted to continue war activities, for this gave them an opportunity to change their fortunes. Navajo Headmen would sign treaties with the Spaniards but tribal members would continue to raid for goods.

As the tribe increased in size and gained more and more livestock, they had to expand their grazing lands. Moving west, they came into conflict with other tribes such as the Hopis, Zunis, Yavapais, Havasupais, and Utes. The problem of insufficient grazing land has continued on into modern times, with never enough land for livestock.

The Spaniards left a mark on this land that remains to this day. They came looking for gold in the 1500s, then colonized the land and stayed for almost 300 years.

Down through the years, treaties between the Spanish Governors and certain Navajo Headmen were signed. They all called for the cessation of warfare, the exchange of prisoners and the transfer of the Indians to another area. They were all broken and the Spanish never understood why the Headmen could not bind the actions of all the other Indians.

Spanish census figures in 1800 indicate that there were 1,500 Zunis, 1,002 Lagunas, 350 Acomas, 798 Hopis and 10,000 Navajos.[39] The Plan of Iguala and the Mexican Declaration of Independence declared that all inhabitants of Mexico were citizens with the right to be employed according to their merit and virtue. The property and person of every citizen was to be respected by the government.[40] The Navajos became citizens of Mexico in 1821, but they soon found that if they resisted any of the programs of the Mexican Government, force was used to bring about compliance. The authorities believed that because the Navajos did not want to live in a community they were barbaric and were a threat to the development of the new government of Mexico.

The bartering system was replaced by the Mexicans with hard currency for all transactions. Navajo children were sold for amounts ranging from 75 to 150 pesos. Sheep also brought a sizable sum. The income from herding and agriculture by the inhabitants of the Rio Grande Valley could never equal the rewards of raiding. In three months of raiding, the income could surpass a lifetime of work. This system made any treaty detrimental to the economy.[41]

The Mexican Government was deeply embittered toward the Navajos, bringing exceedingly cruel actions against them. In the 1830s, a bounty was placed on each Indian scalp, man, woman and child. Headmen were called into a peace conference, then slaughtered by soldiers. At a slave fair, Navajo prisoners were turned over to the Jicarillas, who butchered them on the spot. The Navajos raided Abiqui, Cebolleta, Jemez and Cubero to gain back family members. The government hired Utes, Pueblos and civilians to conduct slave raids for them. These mercenaries were paid in booty which included prisoners and livestock.

There was another attempt at revolt by the Puebloans. In August of 1837 they gathered at La Canada and marched the 25 miles to Sante Fe.

Governor Perez marched to meet the rebels, but was defeated. He was caught in the suburbs and put to death. Secretary of State Alarid was dragged from his house, stripped, scourged, and killed with lances. The replacement governor Armijo chased the rebels out of Sante Fe and defeated them at La Canada. There was no participation by the Navajos and Apaches because they now looked on the Puebloans as enemies. The estimated population at this time was 60,000 Spanish and residents of Spanish descent, 10,000 Puebloans and 10,000 Navajos.[42]

The next years were dominated by repetitive raids and retaliations. There were seven short-lived treaties, mostly unsigned, calling for the exchange of prisoners and the movement of Navajos into settlements or Pueblos. Peace was maintained by all parties in the spring for planting and in summer for growing, but warfare was renewed when the fall harvest was over.

The Spaniards started the slave market but the Mexicans developed it into a full economy. The ability of the Navajos to grow and prosper made them a target for all the peoples in and around the Rio Grande Valley. Mexican citizens adopted the same system that the Navajos used to prosper through raiding. It must have seemed to the Navajos that they stood alone against the world. Those Navajos having the least problems were probably those who moved the farthest west. Those living closest to the Mexicans were raided the most.

Events occurring between the Americans and the Mexicans in other parts of the country would soon have another dramatic impact on the southwestern part of the country.

CHAPTER FIVE

THE YANKEE SOLUTION

It is a well known fact that our country has many reservations for those who are called Native Americans, or more popularly, Indians. All Indian tribes in the United States were either conquered in a war, signed a treaty or were administratively restricted to reservations. They were not given citizenship until 1924. New Mexico passed a law legalizing Indians to drink alcoholic beverages in 1953 and Arizona followed their lead in 1954.

Mexican lands conquered by the United States became a part of this country and the people were considered citizens. Black slaves freed by the civil war and those living in the New England states were considered citizens. Neither of these groups was assigned a reservation.

A reservation is government land set aside for a specific use. The two we are most familiar with are military reservations and Indian reservations. In both instances federal laws, not state laws, prevail. Reservations are exempt from state sales tax. Indians who have adopted their own constitution have certain legal considerations. Indians who have signed treaties have certain legal privileges.

Indians wishing to sign oil leases on their reservation lands must have approval from the Secretary of the Interior. Major crimes such as murder, robbery or other major felonies are under the jurisdiction of the F. B. I. and are prosecuted in federal courts by federal attorneys.

Indians have their own voting system for choosing

their leadership on the reservations which may or may not coincide with state and federal laws.   In the fifties they were finally allowed to vote in state and federal elections.

How is it that the United States has so many Indian Reservations?   How did this come about and why has it continued?   To determine an answer one must look back to the Anglo-Saxon or British mentality which was adopted by their Yankees descendants in the United States before and after the Revolutionary war.

The United States government had many years of experience dealing with Indians in the east, south, west and on the great plains by the time it assumed control of the southwest. The government was convinced that all Indians were nomadic war addicts who misused the land by hunting and gathering food instead of farming it.   So it was deemed fitting that the land should be acquired for proper use by the white men.   If the land was already occupied, it was gained   by conquest and treaty.   If it was not occupied, it was simply appropriated by early settlers or the government.

The term "Yankee" used in this chapter emphasizes that it was primarily those from the former British colonies and new England colonial states who set the foundations for the government of the United States. The Yankees continued the English Colonial System with no thought of "civilizing" the barbarians or converting them to Christianity.   Their only interest was the acquisition of land for colonization.

Indians were never considered as possible members of English society but as separate nations to coexist with through treaties.   English settlers disregarded treaties made by the government with Indians and settled where they pleased, causing constant warfare on the frontiers. The government would then negotiate a new treaty guaranteeing certain lands for

the Indians and establishing a new peace. The treaty
did not restore lands confiscated by settlers.

The Yankees believed that Indians should be
either exterminated or isolated by force and denied
citizenship. As a result of this concept the United
States Government, in 1832, created Indian Territory
west of the Mississippi River where tribes occupying
rich lands in the east could be sent. Once relocated,
the Indians were expected to carry out their lives as
before on these lands given to them by the government. Thousands of Indians were moved to these
lands, creating great hardships. They established
their own form of government without participation by
or interference from the government. Once the
Indians were isolated they could do as they pleased,
as long as they stayed on the lands given them by
the government. Missionaries became interested in
converting them only when they were "tame" enough
for Christianity.

Citizenship was never considered, contrary to the
policy of the Spanish and Mexicans who wanted Indians free to produce goods for commerce and to
supply the slave market as needed. It was possible
for Indians to become citizens of Spain by becoming
Christians, learning a trade, and swearing allegiance
to Spain. The Americans never seriously considered
Indians as a source for slaves because they kept
indentured servants and had black slaves until the
end of the Civil War.

As the Yankees expanded west of the Mississippi
it became evident that there were many more Indians
than the Indian Territory could contain. The concept of reservations became the solution for western
tribes. The Indians were isolated on or near a part
of their originals lands that had no value to the
white settlers and the army kept them there.

Map 3 identifies existing reservations in 1986.
The larger size of the Navajo reservation when
compared to others is evident. The population fig-

ures on the map are not current, as all tribes have increased in population. It is noteworthy that six of the ten largest tribes are located in the state of Arizona.

MAP 3:   NATIVE AMERICAN RESERVATIONS

Source:"Native American Reservations, 10 most-populated are numbered," The Arizona Republic, September, 1993.

The Indians were forced to sign a peace treaty that contained the provision that they remain on the reservation in return for army protection from the settlers and some payment in cash and in the necessities of life. The Indians were used to hunting and gathering food over a large area of land and a limited reservation could not support them. The government would agree to support them temporarily until they could become self-sufficient through cattle raising or farming. These solutions never became realities due to the poor land on which the Indians were forced to live.

An excellent word picture of the Navajos, before the United States conquered New Mexico, was created by an American newspaper reporter who visited Sante Fe during the Mexican period and wrote the following description:

"They have fine flocks of sheep, abundance of mules and herds of cattle of a superior kind. They have gardens and peach orchards. Several articles of their woolen manufacture equal the quality of ours"...

`Navajos wore blankets draped over one shoulder... and short trousers' "which came halfway down the calf and were split at the knee. `Some of the trousers were made of Spanish cloth, others of soft "excellently tanned" buckskin. Clothing...was "decorated along the seams with silver buttons."

...`Navajo women'..."wore a double--blanket dress of woolen material, fastened at the shoulders and hanging down front and back. It provided freedom of movement for working about a cooking fire, herding sheep, or riding. Their jewelry consisted of turquoise, corral, silver pendants, bracelets, necklaces, and buttons." [43]

The United States and Mexico fought a bitter war from 1846 to 1848. One action of this war was the occupation of Sante Fe by General Stephen W. Kearney on August 18th, 1846. He maintained Sante Fe as a capital.

The Navajos were totally unprepared for the "Yankee Solution" concerning Indians. When the army marched into Sante Fe, there was no indication of the tremendous resources behind the army and the Navajos probably felt that this was just one more change in government and that life would be as usual.

After visiting with the local citizens for four days General Kearney accepted their stories of savage Indians and issued a public proclamation to protect all the quiet and peaceful inhabitants of the Rio Grande Valley. The General admired the Pueblo people for they lived in small, compact villages, farmed their lands, and lived as civilized people should. They were the model that all Indians should emulate. It was obvious that the good citizens convinced the Army of Occupation that they were indeed the civilized ones and that the Navajos were barbarians.

Kearney authorized Mexican and Pueblo citizens to form war parties for the purpose of recovering their property, making reprisals and seeking redress against the Indians. His order not to harm the elderly, women and children was promptly ignored by the raiders.

Even though the area was not yet a part of the United States, General Kearney initiated the first steps of American policy concerning Indians by inviting all Navajo Headmen to a conference to negotiate a treaty. The Navajos ignored him so he ordered Colonel Alexander W. Doniphan and the Missouri Mounted Volunteers to recover all stolen property, including Mexican and other prisoners, from the Indians, and to restore them to the citizens of New Mexico. Colonel Doniphan was to use any necessary measures to accomplish the task, including the taking of hostages.

Occupational Governor Bent informed the Secretary of State that the warfare had gone on for many years and that New Mexico could never prosper until the Navajos were subdued. He complained that many Navajos were wealthier than some of the honorable citizens.

From 1846 to 1862 life continued much as before for the Navajos. They expanded their raiding expeditions to include northern Mexico. The same people raided them. The soldiers made punitive expeditions into their lands and then returned to the Rio Grande Valley. Treaties were signed and peace was observed while planting and harvesting were accomplished. Then the raids would begin again. Those Navajos who were not represented for treaty negotiations ignored them.

The army's attitude was obvious when 40 horses were taken by Navajos. Soldiers were ordered to scalp the culprits, if caught, and if that was not possible, to appropriate 40 horses from any Indian that could be found.

Colonel Doniphan and Major William Gilpin presented the first treaty to a group of Navajo Headmen at Bear Springs. Narbona, Sarcillos Largo, Caballada de Mucho, Alexandro, Sandoval, Capitanito and Jose Largo signed that treaty with the United States. These headmen were from the bands closest to Sante Fe, the ones who usually signed treaties with the Mexicans. The treaty provided for peace and a mutual exchange of prisoners taken since the arrival of Americans in New Mexico. The treaty was never ratified by the U. S. Senate.[44]

The New Mexicans held the American soldiers in contempt. Many of the military volunteers from the Midwest were uneducated, dirty and rowdy, and daily insulted the inhabitants. They openly violated the

laws.   The Americans mistakenly thought that, because they defended the Mexican and Puebloan people
against the Navajos, their actions would end the
hatred directed at them.

Military heads sent the best of the army's fighting men to Mexico to help with the war, but they were
replaced by inexperienced and untrained state militiamen. The Mexicans and Puebloans recognized this
weakness in the army and revolted on January 19,
1847.   They killed the governor but by February were
defeated at Taos. One rebel leader was hanged and
another killed while in custody.

Major J. G. Walker commanded the first military
campaign against the Navajos on September 10, 1847.
A battalion of American soldiers, an undetermined
number of Mexicans, several Puebloan scouts and a
battery of field artillery traveled west to Bear
Springs and on to Canyon de Chelly in a vain search
for Navajos.   The Navajos were impressed with this
show of force and sent a delegation of headmen to
Sante Fe to discuss peace and to agree to the terms
of the Bear Springs Treaty. They were well received
and they agreed to keep their warriors home for five
months, but by March, the raids against the villages
began again.[45]

The United States and Mexico ratified the Treaty
of Guadalupe Hidalgo on May 30, 1848 which gave the
United States all of the territory west of the Rio
Grande River.   When the treaty was proclaimed on the
following August in Sante Fe, it meant that the Navajos were now the official responsibility of the
United States, but not citizens.

Colonel E. W. C. Newbury immediately negotiated
another treaty at Beautiful Mountain with Jose Largo,
Narbona, Chapatone, Zarcillos Largos, Archuleta, Juan
Lucero, Secundo and Pablo Pino.   The provisions of
this treaty called for peace, mutual trade, mutual
visitation, exchange of prisoners, guaranteed observ-
ance of the treaty by the people of New Mexico, and a

payment of 300 head of sheep and 100 mules and horses
to be made to the United States. This treaty, as
others before it, was never ratified by the U.S.
Senate.[46]

In 1849, James S. Calhoun was appointed as the
first Indian Agent in New Mexico. Within two months
after his appointment, Calhoun and Colonel John Mac-
Crae Washington led a second major campaign against
the Navajos. They proceeded through Torreon, Pueblo
Pintada, Chaco Canyon, Tunicha Mountains, through a
mountain pass(later to be named Washington Pass) and
on to Canyon de Chelly. There were many Navajos in
the area.

Narbona, a great advocate of peace, was killed by
troops in a skirmish over a stolen horse. Several
other Indians were killed, houses were burned, 242
horses and a large amount of corn were seized by the
army. In spite of this tense situation, a treaty was
negotiated after two weeks.[47]

The terms of the newest treaty called upon the
Navajos to recognize the sovereignty of the United
States, keep the peace, allow the regulation of
trade, surrender the murderers of a Micente Garcia,
exchange prisoners and all property taken by the
Navajos; the government would punish citizens who
committed crimes against the Navajos, provide free
passage through the Navajo lands, and reduce Navajo
land boundaries. This treaty was ratified by the
U. S. Senate on September 9, 1850 and proclaimed by
the President of the United States on September 24,
1850.[48]

The peace was short-lived, for Navajo raids were
reported from Cebolleta to Valverde during the next
year. A private Mexican expedition went as far as
Black Mountain and captured 5,000 head of livestock
and 52 slaves.

Soon after this event Congress declared New Mexico
a territory, which included Arizona. In 1851 Agent

Calhoun estimated that the Navajos had captured
150,231 sheep, 893 horses, 761 mules and 1,234 cows
since the Americans had occupied New Mexico. This
was a blatantly gross exaggeration and assumed that
only Navajos were raiding the settlements.

A group of Navajos and Puebloans living around
Mount Taylor and Pueblo Pintada earned the name of
"Traitor Navajos" because of their dealing with the
Mexicans, Puebloans, and now Americans. Sandoval,
their headman, sold Navajos in the slave markets of
Albuquerque and Sante Fe. Governor Calhoun reported
to the commissioner that:

> "Sandoval, our Navajo friend near
> Cebolleta, returned about the 20th
> of the month from a visit to his
> Navajo brethren with 18 captives, a
> quantity of stock and several scalps,
> having lost one man in the expedi-
> tion. . ."[49]

Colonel Edwin Vose Sumner assumed command of the
Ninth Military Department in New Mexico in 1851. He
immediately established a fort at the mouth of Canyon
Bonito and named it Fort Defiance. It was dubbed
"Hell's Gate" by troopers stationed there. The
Colonel felt that if this did not stop the raiding,
then the Navajos must be exterminated.

Records show that the Americans proposed another
Indian Treaty. The commander of Fort Defiance, Major
Electus Backus, signed one with the local headmen.
Another treaty was signed at the Pueblo of Jemez
between Colonel Sumner and the Navajos but these
treaties were never ratified, and no copies of them
have ever been found.

The raiding and slavery system caused many hardships for the Navajos. At a peace meeting in Sante
Fe a well known Navajo Headman named Armijo stated
his desires for peace for the following reasons:

"My people are crying in the same
way. Three of our chiefs now sitting before you mourn for their children who have been taken from their
homes by the Mexicans. More than 200
of our children have been carried
off and we know not where they are.
The Mexicans have lost but few children in comparison with what they have
stolen from us. Three years ago they
took from my people nearly all
their horses. Two years ago my
brother lost 700 animals. How shall
we get them again? From the time of
Colonel Newbury we have been trying to
get our children back again. Eleven
times have we given our captives--only
once have they given us ours. My
people are yet crying for the children
they have lost....I have lost my
grandfather and two other members of
my family who were all killed by
Mexicans. I have never sought revenge. My hair is beginning to get
gray. I wish to live in peace with
everyone."[50]

Other headmen in attendance were Barbon, Black
Eagle, Hosea Miguel, Luke Lea, Raffaille, Charvis and
Wingfield Scott. Slavery continued to flourish and
in 1852 Navajo children were being led around the
country like beasts by Mexicans who were peddling
them for prices ranging from $40 to $120. The children were as young as 6 and as old as 18. In 1853,
Captain H.L. Kendrick was of the opinion that the
best way to handle the Navajos would be to give them
to the Mexicans as their slaves.

By 1854 Navajos were raiding as far south as
Chihuahua and Durango in Mexico. Mounted Navajos had
access to the whole southwest and northern Mexico.
By 1856 the Mormons near the Hopi Villages were
trading silver mounted rifles, blankets and tobacco

with the Navajos.

Because he assumed that the Navajos had a single ruler, Governor Meriwether issued a medal of office and appointed Sarcillos Largos as chief of the Navajos. In 1855 Sarcillos Largos had a representative return his medal and inform the governor that he was resigning as chief. Manuelito was then elected by the headmen who signed the treaty to be their spokesman.[51]

Henry L. Dodge was a very popular Agent among the Navajos. He tried to learn their language and customs and tried several solutions to their plight. It was rumored that he had a Navajo wife and children. He traveled in safety among the Navajos. Agent Dodge was killed by Apaches while hunting with Navajo friends near Zuni Salt Lake.

An American report in 1857 estimated that the Navajos could turn out 2,000 to 3,000 warriors at any given time and that there were 12,000 Navajos living in the territory. Had it been true that the Navajos could field so many warriors, the Mexicans and Utes would not have continued to raid them.

Navajos killed a black slave of the commanding officer of Fort Defiance and the army was sent to chastise them. Sarcillos Largos was wounded in a battle at Red Lake, north of Fort Defiance, by army troops. The captain of the troops commended the headman for his bravery and courage in battle. Colonel Dixon Stansbury Miles summed up the result of the campaign: 60 Navajos dead, many times that wounded, 25 prisoners, 250 horses and 13,000 sheep confiscated. He felt that the army had humbled the Navajos by marching through their lands and destroying their homes. It seems that the Spaniards and Mexicans were not the only ones prone to exaggeration.

Colonels B. L. E. Bonneville and J. L. Collins negotiated another treaty with fifteen headmen including Manuelito, Armijo, Ganado Mucho and others.

The provisions of the treaty reduced the east boundary of the Navajo lands, called for the payment of an
indemnity by the tribe for past sins, requested an
exchange of prisoners, and pardoned the murderers of
the black slave. This treaty was not ratified by the
U. S. Senate.

The Mexicans found it easy to claim losses suppos-
edly caused by Navajos, for the government never
investigated Indian raids. Retaliation was always
against the Navajos, regardless of who raided the
settlements.

In 1860 Navajos attacked Fort Defiance but were
driven off after killing one trooper. In August a
fort was established at Bear Springs called Fort
Fauntleroy, after the Commandant of New Mexico. It
was later changed to Fort Wingate in honor of an
officer killed in the battle of Valverde during the
Civil War.

Zuni raiders killed Sarcillos Largos in 1860 on
the south side of Canyon de Chelly. The Zunis were
now participating in stealing animals and material
wealth from the prosperous Navajos.

And still another treaty was negotiated in February of 1861. It was negotiated at Fort Fauntleroy by
Major Ed R. S. Canby with 49 Navajo Headmen. Among
those were Barboncito, Manuelito, Armijo and Ganado
Mucho. These headmen were becoming very good at
treaties, as they were constantly being called to
meetings by the army. This one contained the usual
provisions for land changes, the exchange of prisoners, and peace. The headmen were required to establish pueblos for their people. They were to report
their success at a council in May. This treaty was
not ratified by the U. S. Senate.[52]

The United States authorities refused to accept
the fact that the Navajo didn't have "chiefs" or
"rulers." They could not understand the clan and
family systems. A young man could raid the Rio

Grande Valley populations for sheep, horses , cattle and slaves to become an important man. Those who were poor ignored the headmen and the treaties they signed. The headmen wanted to negotiate peace to protect their belongings but they didn't represent the feelings of all of the Navajos.

Major Canby of Fort Defiance was the first American officer to recognize the Mexican aggressions against the Navajos. He reported wanton seizure of the property of the Navajos, including those who were friendly to the United States.

The Civil War began in 1861 and many professional soldiers were transferred from the territories in the west to the battle fields of the east. Fort Defiance was abandoned in May and the Mexican, Ute and Puebloan raiders converged on the lands of the Navajos. The Navajos retaliated and the land was plunged into bitter warfare. Slavery flourished with small children selling for $300 in 1862.[53]

Major Canby was transferred east and General James Henry Carleton became the district military commander in the fall of 1862. Carleton's burning desire was to settle the Indian problem once and for all using the familiar traditional method. He immediately requested agricultural land to be set aside as a reservation, the construction of a fort, troops to guard against plundering of the captives and to prevent Indian prisoners from escaping.

His solution was simple: put the hostile Navajos and Apaches on a reservation, make them farmers and they would become productive citizens who could manage for themselves, making it possible for white people to settle on the unoccupied land and make it productive. Better yet, he would win national recognition for this fantastic solution. He disregarded the fact that a reservation system had been in use for over a hundred years without any success. Both the Department of Indian Affairs and the Department of War agreed with the plan. The proposed reservation was to be on the Pecos River in New Mexico where groves of cottonwood trees stretched for sixteen miles along the river, and was called "Bosque Redondo" or "round groves".

A board of army officers was sent to inspect the location. The members were critical because the site was so far from army supply depots and forage. Building materials would have to be freighted from great distances. The water also contained unhealthful minerals. The surrounding valley was subject to spring floods and would be completely inundated. Carleton overruled the board and the War Department sided with him. The Civil War was creating a shortage of soldiers in the west. The Carleton solution would use various state voluntary militiamen to make up for the loss of regular army troops.

The new fort was to be named after General Edwin Vose Sumner. With the establishment of a reservation, Governor Connelly issued the following proclamation:

> "For many years you have been suffering from hostile inroads of a perfidious tribe of Indians, who notwithstanding the efforts of the government to ameliorate their condition and administer to their wants in every respect, do not cease daily to encroach upon the rights and depreciate upon the lives and property of the peaceful citizens of New Mexico. For a long series of years have we been subjected to the rapacity and desolation of this hostile tribe, which has reduced many a wealthy citizen to poverty, and the greater part of our citizens to want and mendacity; which has murdered hundreds of our people, and carried out women and children into captivity. Almost every family

in the territory has to mourn the
loss of some loved one who has been
made to sacrifice his life to these
bloodthirsty Navajos. Our highways
are insecure, and the entire country
is now invaded and overrun by these
rapacious Indians, murdering, robbing
and carrying off whatever may come
in their way. Such a state of
things cannot and must not longer be
endured."[54]

The governor ordered the New Mexico militia to
reorganize and be ready to march into the Navajo
country by October of 1862. This was to be a sus-
tained and victorious campaign against the Navajos.
In previous wars the groups passed through Navajo
territory, gathered captives and goods, and returned
to the Rio Grande Valley. Most of the Navajos left
their homes and simply hid out until the raiders
left. The concept of continuous campaigns lasting
for a long period of time in their lands was outside
of their experience or imagination.

The other Indians such as the Utes, Paiutes,
Zunis, Hopis and Apaches saw this as an opportunity
for material gains and eagerly volunteered to assist
in the campaign.

CHAPTER SIX

CONQUEST AND IMPRISONMENT

When Arizona became a territory on February 24, 1863, Charles W. Poston was appointed as the Indian Agent. He and other officials made their headquarters near Prescott. Although most of the Navajos lived in this new territory, these events had little impact on them.

General Carleton began his campaign by capturing the Mescalero Apaches, raiders who lived on lands coveted by others. In a few short months 400 Mescalero Apaches were removed to Bosque Redondo in New Mexico where they were forced to till the soil under the direction of the American soldiers.

It was May of 1863 before General Carleton was ready to implement the Navajo campaign and ordered troops to Fort Wingate. He authorized a prize of $20 for every horse and $1 for every sheep confiscated by volunteers. The Ute, Hopi, Zuni and Pueblo tribes supplied scouts. An undetermined number of Mexicans rushed to raid the Navajos. They were armed and supplied by the army and it must have been like a dream come true. No doubt many citizens became wealthy property owners as a direct result of this campaign.

There were innumerable raids upon the Navajos from all sides. The California Volunteers manned forts outside the Navajo country and kept the Apaches busy so that they could not go to the aide of their previous tribal members.[55]

General Carleton's General Order Number 15 was issued on June 15, 1863 from Sante Fe, New Mexico. Carleton's policy was very clear: All captives who

MAP 4:   FORTS AROUND NAVAJOS IN 1864

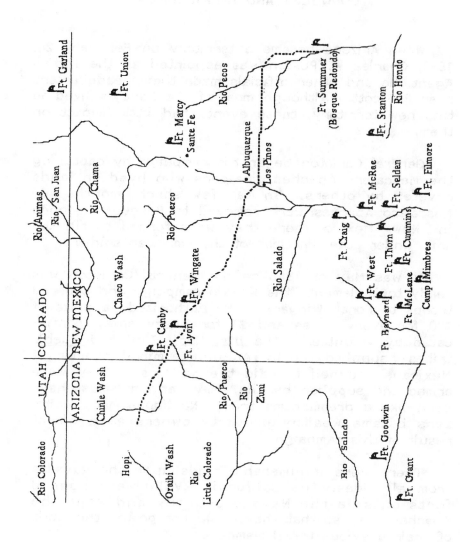

surrendered   voluntarily would be taken to Fort
Sumner and all males who resisted would be shot.

Colonel Christopher Carson had orders to take a
proper military force and proceed to a point in
Navajo country known as Pueblo Colorado where he
would establish a defensible supply depot and a
hospital. This new post was to be named Fort Canby
in honor of a recent commander of the War Department of New Mexico.

Pueblo Colorado was the name of the area now
called Ganado, Arizona. Lorenzo Hubbell changed
the name in the 1870's to honor Ganado Mucho, a
famed Navajo Headman of the area, and to avoid the
confusion with the city of Pueblo, in the state of
Colorado.   Some   written   records still confuse the
proposed location of Fort Canby as being in Pueblo,
Colorado.

Most of Colonel Carson's staff officers were from
the First New Mexico Volunteers. Captain A. B.
Carey, the chief quartermaster, was regular army
and the chief of the commissary was from the First
Infantry California Volunteers. Colonel Carson went
into the field with 2 mountain howitzers on prairie
carriages, enough ammunition to defend the depot at
Pueblo Colorado, 9 companies of men containing 406
cavalry, and 260 foot soldiers.[56] Lieutenant Colonel
Chaves of the First New Mexico Volunteers was to
garrison Fort Wingate with 4 companies containing
84 mounted troopers and 242 foot soldiers.

Colonel Carson arrived with the first four companies at Pueblo Colorado in July. The other troops
had many problems and did not arrive in force until
October of that year. The Colonel had great faith
in his Ute scouts and asked for thirty more. His first
act was to seize all of the wheat and corn in the
vicinity for his horses. He next asked that Fort
Canby be moved from Pueblo Colorado due to the
lack of timber, water and grazing for the horses. He
was given permission to move to the abandoned Fort

Defiance and to rename it Fort Canby.

Colonel Carson's first scouting expedition in August traveled south to the Zuni Villages, northwest to the Hopi Villages and then east, returning by the way of Canyon de Chelly. It lasted 27 days and covered an estimated 490 miles with very little contact with the Navajos. Some of the Ute scouts had taken captives and left for home. General Carleton was upset and ordered Carson to turn all captives over to troops to be taken to Fort Sumner. The Colonel complained about the Hopis warning the Navajos of his troop movements through their country and asked that they be moved to Fort Sumner also.

Colonel Carson did not feel that a winter campaign would be effective so he asked Carleton for two months leave to visit his family. He had been gone from his home, except for brief visits, since May of 1861. Carleton denied his request and ordered him to take the field against the Navajos. He further stipulated that when Carson had captured 100 Navajos he could bring them and the prisoners at Fort Wingate to Fort Sumner. When this task was completed he would then be allowed to visit his home in New Mexico.

There were no maps of Canyon de Chelly nor did anyone other than Navajos know its dimensions. Colonel Carson planned to begin the campaign in December but due to changes in officers and other problems had to postpone it until January 6, 1864. He began the campaign with 14 officers and 375 enlisted men, in deep snow and bitterly cold weather.

The Canyon de Chelly campaign lasted for 16 days and when Carson returned to Fort Canby he had killed 23 Navajos, taken 34 prisoners and received over 200 Navajos who surrendered voluntarily. Colonel Carson's policy to release Navajo prisoners who would talk their bands into surrendering was

successful. He was able to convince them that the
troops under his command would not harm them or
those who surrendered and that they all would be
fed. More Navajos came in each day due to the
cold weather and their lack of food and lodging.
Carson's men burned corn and dried foods, destroyed homes and all of the orchards they could
find. By the end of January, as a result of the
campaign, there were over 1200 prisoners at Fort
Canby.

The first group on the long walk to Bosque
Redondo began their trek on February 14, in the
middle of winter. There were 1,445 Navajos in that
march. By early March there were over 2,500 Navajos at Fort Canby, but on the way to Bosque Redondo
323 of them died of the cold and dysentery.

The beginning of the end for the Navajos was
indicated by the large number of people who voluntarily surrendered each day. So many people were
coming in that the army could not provide adequate
food, blankets or shelter and many of the prisoners
either died or ran away.

General Carleton wanted to complete the project.
He insisted that the 8,000 people at Bosque Redondo
were all of the Navajos and refused to pursue any
further campaigns to the west. Colonel Carson
indicated that his Indian scouts reported that there
were wealthy Navajos living southeast and southwest
of the Little Colorado River and in the Apache
country. He estimated that 6,000 Navajos remained
free. Manuelito's band, who evaded troopers long
after the others surrendered, reported that over 800
Navajos had made peace with the Wimenuche Utes
and joined them in the North.[57]

Governor Connelly declared an end to the hostili-
ties on May 4th, 1864. General Carleton had issued
his General Order Number 15 on June 15, 1863 and
in eleven months over 8,000 Navajos had been made
prisoners and marched to Fort Sumner. In less than

a   year's time the majority of the Navajos had been conquered.

Kit Carson was a man in the right place at the right time to become a legend in the history of the southwest.   He has been glamorized in movies and stories as a buckskin clad Indian fighter and scout.   In reality, he was a career army officer stationed on the frontier. He married Josefa Jaramillo, a Spanish woman from a wealthy family and lived in Taos, New Mexico, when he was able to go home.

His knowledge of the Indians was remarkable. He worked with many and fought many others. He had a close relationship with the Utes living in Colorado who served him faithfully as scouts in the campaign against the Navajos. His last active assignment was in Colorado working with the Utes.

He understood the Navajos well and knew their major weaknesses. He effectively destroyed their crops, animals and homes, forcing them to surrender. Due to his expertise, some 8,000 Navajos were overcome by less than 800 men. He was repulsed by the fate of the Navajos and at times tried to put Navajos into Mexican homes rather than condemning them to the horrors of Fort Sumner.

Colonel Carson was assigned to Fort Sumner in the Spring of 1864, but was bitterly disappointed when the army's restrictions made it impossible to work effectively with the Navajos. He asked for a discharge which was denied. After he submitted his request three times he was reassigned in September of 1864.   The Colonel served against the Kiowas and Comanches until he was reassigned to Fort Garland in Colorado in August of 1866. He served in this post until November 27, 1867 when he finally received his discharge from the army. He died on May 25, 1868 at Fort Lyon, Colorado. A year later his body and that of his wife were moved from Colorado to Taos, New Mexico for reburial.[58]

ILLUSTRATION 4: BOSQUE REDONDO

Source: Underhill, Ruth, *Here Come the Navajo*, Lawrence: Haskell Institute Press, January, 1953. 159.

2.   Peonage was still authorized by statute in New Mexico.

3.   Although the enslavement of Indians was illegal, it was widely practiced. Thousands of Indians were being held by the officials and citizens of New Mexico and slavery raids were being conducted at Fort Sumner.

4.   Slavery was an excuse for many acts of vengeance on the Navajos.

5.   The commissary of the war department had ordered provisions of such poor quality that they were declared unfit for the soldiers but sent to Bosque Redondo for the Navajos.

6.   Large quantities of supplies and equipment disappeared between the point of purchase and Fort Sumner.

7.   The Comanches were raiding the reservation because the army was not protecting the Navajos from them.

8.   The livestock that the Navajos had been encouraged to bring with them had been run off by the Comanches and Mexicans.

9.   More than a thousand Navajos had run away to escape starvation and abuse.

10.   The hospital was inadequate and was feared by the Navajos because of their belief in death avoidance, and venereal disease outnumbered all other diseases.

11.   The water of the Pecos River was highly impregnated with alkali and other minerals causing dysentery and threatening the health of the captives.

12.   All fuel adjacent to the area had been used and the Navajos walked as far as twenty miles to

gather mesquite roots which they carried home on their backs.

13. Both soil and water were unsuitable for agriculture.

14. The $100,000 appropriated by Congress annually for the upkeep of the Navajos paid for only a small part of their needs.

15. The War Department had no acceptable excuse for the improper care for the Navajos.[60]

The report created a furor in Washington between the government agencies and Congress. General Carleton was relieved of his command in September and in 1867 the President turned over the custody of the Navajos to the Department of Indian Affairs.[61]

There were approximately 7,304 Navajos on the reservation. Several hundred had died of hunger and disease, some had been carried off into slavery and others had escaped to return to their old lands.

On the 28th of May, 1868, General W. T. Sherman and Colonel Samuel F. Tappan met with a delegation of headmen composed of Delgadito, Barboncito, Manuelito, Largo, Herrero, Armijo and Torivio. James Sutherland translated from English to Spanish and Jesus Arviso translated from Spanish to Navajo. General Sherman stated that they were there to learn all about the conditions of the Navajos and wanted only to hear the truth. He indicated that the government had given the land to them with materials and supplies, but that there were no farms and the Navajos looked as poor as they had been four years earlier. General Sherman stated that he wanted to know what had been done in the past and what the Navajos thought of their reservation.

Barboncito replied that being brought to the reservation had caused many people to die. He said

that he did not think it was right to ask them to
live anywhere except in their own country. He added
that the ground at Fort Sumner was not productive
for when it was planted it did not yield a crop. The
Navajos knew how to farm but they could not raise
a crop here. Continuing, he said that nearly all of
their sheep and horses had died or had been stolen
from them, and then said:

> "It seems that whatever we do
> here causes death, some workers at
> the acquias take sick and die, others
> die with a hoe in their hands, they
> go to the river up to their waists
> and suddenly disappear. Others have
> been struck and torn to pieces with
> lightning. A rattlesnake bite here
> kills us, in our own country a rat-
> tlesnake before he bites gives
> warning which enables us to keep out
> of its way and if bitten we readily
> find a cure--- here we can find no
> cure."[62]

Barboncito further pointed out that when they
came, there were plenty of mesquite roots for fire-
wood, but now they had to walk 25 miles to get
wood and many died from the cold, sickness and
the overexertion of carrying wood such a long distance on their backs. He told how the Comanches
and Mexicans killed the men and drove off their livestock.

The Yankee policy was to isolate Indians by
sending them to Indian Territory in Kansas or to
create a reservation near their homeland but only
on land that was not desired by others. General
Sherman offered to send some of the leaders to
Indian Territory south of Kansas to see if they
wanted to live on a reservation there. He also promised that they could return to their own country
but that only a portion of their original land would

be available.

The Navajos were at least given a chance to select some of their original homelands instead of being compelled to live in Indian Territory. They had been forced to go to Fort Sumner and they wanted to return to their home. Barboncito replied;

> "I hope to God you will not ask me to go to any other country except my own. It might turn out another Bosque Redondo. They told us this was a good place when we came but it is not."[63]

The council met again on May 29th with all of the Navajos assembled. General Sherman cited the previous discussions, telling the people that they had been given two choices, and that Barboncito had insisted upon going back to their own country. He asked them to appoint ten delegates to represent them during the discussions and to sign the treaty. Selected delegates were Delgadito, Barboncito, Manuelito, Largo, Herrero, Chiqueto, Muerto de Hombre, Hombro, Narbona and Armijo. These men were then asked to select a chief for the council and Barboncito was unanimously elected.

General Sherman asked the assembled people if they wanted schools in their country. Barboncito said that they wanted to return to their original home but did not know about the group from the Cebolletas. He requested permission to hunt and trade outside the reservation boundaries. General Sherman agreed but said that they could neither farm nor build homes outside of the reservation.

Barboncito then said...

> "After we get back to our country, it will brighten up again and the Navajos will be happy as the land, black clouds will rise and there

will be plenty of rain. Corn will grow
in   abundance   and everything will
look happy.   Today is a   day   that
anything black or red   does not look
right, every thing should   be white
or yellow representing   the flower of
the corn."[64]

Barboncito requested that the Mexicans return all
Navajo captives to their families. General Sherman
assured him that   the Indians   would   have legal
recourse for the return of   their   relatives.   Barboncito asked that a blacksmith and carpenter's shop   be
established on the reservation.   When General Sherman asked if   the assembly   wanted schools in their
country, Barboncito replied   that if   schools were
established, the children would attend after   they
were settled. General Sherman promised to do all that
he could to get   their children returned to them.   On
this positive   note,   the council adjourned.

On May 30th, the proposed treaty was read to the
ten   headmen who   asked that two more men be
appointed to the council.   General Sherman   agreed
to let Narbona Segundo and Ganado Mucho   join   the
council.   Sherman asked if Fort Defiance would be
acceptable as   an agency and that site was agreed
upon.

On   Monday, the first of June, 1868, the council
met   again to sign   the   treaty, a classic example of
the "Yankee   Solution"   for treating   Indians as a
conquered foreign nation. The articles   of the   treaty
contained the following general provisions: "From
this   day forward all war   between the parties of
this agreement shall forever cease." [65]

Article One was the agreement   between   both
parties   to cease warfare, with provisions   for each
side to punish those breaking the law.

Article Two defined the area of the   reservation,
with statements that the government could allow

other friendly tribes or individuals to reside there. It also defined those who would be permitted to pass over, settle on, or reside in this territory in the discharge of lawful duties.

In Article Three, the United States agreed to establish an Agency Headquarters, with limited funding. Included were allowances for a warehouse ($2,500) the Agency building ($3,000) carpenter's shop ($1,000) and a blacksmith shop ($1,000); also promised were a schoolhouse, when there were enough children willing to attend, and a chapel ($5,000).

Article Four provided for an Agency head to live at the headquarters and maintain regular office hours.

Article Five gave 160 acres of farming land to each family head, and 80 acres to all others over eighteen, each transaction to be recorded in a Land Book.

In Article Six, the government promised a classroom and a teacher for every 30 children aged 6 to 16, with attendance to be enforced by the Agent.

Article Seven provided land holders with $100 worth of seeds and farming tools for the first year, and $25 for the next two years.

Article Eight stated that for the next ten years, on the first day of September, $5 worth of clothing, goods or raw materials was to be available to each Navajo. An annual census by the Agent would be used to estimate needs each year. An additional $10 per person was to be allotted for other expenses, determined by the Commissioner of Indian Affairs. All distributions were to be monitored by an Officer of the Army.

In Article Nine, the Navajos agreed neither to oppose the building or passage of railroads on their lands, nor to attack people at home or traveling, wagons, coaches or livestock. They agreed never again to capture women or children or to kill, scalp or harm men. The construction of roads, railways, mail station, and utilities would no longer be opposed. Damage to the land would be recompensed by the Government as assessed by a commission which would include a headman.

Article Ten stated that no other treaties or changes to the treaty would be enacted without the approval of three-fourths of the adult Navajo males concerned.

Article Eleven allowed the transportation of the Indians to the reservation, with the government to be responsible for their subsistence and for the transportation of the sick and feeble.

Article Twelve asked for the appropriation of $150,000 to transport the Navajos to the reservation ($50,000), to buy 15,000 head of sheep and goats ($30,000), to buy 500 head of beef cattle and 1,000,000 pounds of corn for use in the approaching winter, and the remainder for the maintenance of the Indians, pending their removal. It also provided that the move was to be undertaken by the Military Commander of the Territory of New Mexico and then revert to the proper Indian Agent.

In Article Thirteen, the Navajos were to agree to live within the prescribed boundaries of the reservation; they would be allowed to hunt in the adjoining land; any Indian choosing to leave would forfeit all rights, privileges and annuities conferred by the treaty.

Twenty nine Headmen made their mark on the treaty. The Senate ratified this treaty on the first day of June, 1868, and President Andrew Johnson accepted and confirmed the treaty on the 25th day of July.[66]

It still remains in effect and has never been
modified by any mutual act of the United States and
the Navajo Nation. In effect, this treaty made the
Navajos members of a separate Navajo Nation who
were not granted United States citizenship until 1924,
giving them dual citizenship.

CHART 4: TREATIES BETWEEN THE UNITED STATES AND
THE NAVAJO NATION

Date	Location	Representative	Congressional Action
1846	Bear Springs	Colonel Doniphan Major Gilpin	Never Ratified by Congress.
5/13/1848 Treaty of Guadalupe Hidalgo Between Mexico and the United States made the southwest a part of the United States.			
1848	Beautiful Mountain	Colonel Newbury	Never Ratified by Congress
1849	Canyon de Chelly	Indian Agent James C. Calhoun	Ratified by Congress 9/9/1850 Signed by President 9/26/1850
1850 New Mexico becomes a Territory.			
1851	Fort Defiance	Major Backus	Never Ratified, lost.
	Jemez Pueblo	Colonel Sumner	Never Ratified, lost.
1858	Fort Defiance	Colonel Bonneville Colonel Collins	Never Ratified by Congress
1861	Fort Fauntleroy	Major Canby	Never Ratified by Congress
1863 Arizona becomes a separate Territory			
1864 Navajos Imprisoned at Fort Sumner, New Mexico.			
1868	Fort Sumner	General Sheridan Colonel Tappan	Ratified by Senate 6/1/1868 Signed by President 7/25/1868

CHAPTER SEVEN

RETURN TO A RESERVATION

After years of deprivation and suffering, the Navajos were finally allowed to return to a portion of their former lands. The new Navajo reservation was approximately 3.5 million acres or about one fifth of the territory that had been their traditional homeland. The government placed the agency headquarters in an area previously built as an army fort to control the flow of Navajo raiders from the regions west of Canyon Bonito. It would have been much more effective and sensible to place the new agency at Canyon de Chelly, the geographical center of the original Navajo lands. The Navajos were held in the vicinity of Fort Defiance because that was where the rations and seeds were doled out by the Indian Agent. Those who wished to live in the old traditional ways had to travel great distances to get their rations and supplies.

The ancestors of the Canoncito Navajos moved southward to the Cebolleta Mountains instead of westward with the rest of the tribe. They were more aligned with the Spaniards, Mexicans and the Americans than their own people. As the procession of 7,000 Navajos marched out of Albuquerque, about 400 people separated and their headman Delgadito led them home to the Cebolleta region.

Another group made their way west and north of Socorro to the Magdalena and Ladron Mountains. Some of their kinsmen had remained in that region when Colonel Carson was rounding up the rest of the Navajos. Probably some of the escapees from Fort Sumner also joined this group.

Eventually this land was purchased by the gov-

ernment and the Navajo Tribe for this group of
Navajos. Some Navajos had escaped to live with the
Chiricahua Apaches and formed a community near a
spring at Ramah. Other returning captives left the
main group near Fort Wingate and wintered there.
They proceeded on to Ramah in the spring to join
their kinsmen.

The Navajos returned to their traditional homes
without regard to the treaty reservation. Many continued on to the west where relatives and clan
members had remained during their period of captivity. In a very short time after returning to their
lands many Navajos had moved back into the remote
strongholds of previous times. Those who returned
to the area nearest to Fort Defiance found ruined
orchards, burned homes and desolated lands. They
were totally dependent upon the government for
survival. Others, after receiving their rations, seeds
and livestock moved to the west and the north.

During the four years of terrible stress and
hardship at Fort Sumner, the singers or medicine men
became very strong and were respected by all of the
Navajos. For the first time, they were in a position
to observe and interact with each other. The ceremonies could be practiced under the scrutiny of all of
the singers. They exchanged different versions of
the   myths and ceremonies to develop commonly
accepted ones. This collaboration had the effect of
strengthening the religious beliefs and customs of the
Navajos instead of diminishing them as their captors
had hoped. The practice of witchcraft also increased
and became a tool of many Hatathlies for controlling
people.

Many problems faced the Navajos in the following
years but their return to their traditional lands
helped them to endure. Barboncito admonished all of
the people not to break the peace and offered this
advice:

ILLUSTRATION 5:   NAVAJO CAMP AFTER IMPRISONMENT

Source: Underhill, Ruth, *Here Come the Navajo*, Lawrence: Haskell Institute Press,
January, 1953. 196.

Laboratory of Anthropology

"We lost everything. Tell that to
your children. See that they do not
fight. See that they work. Take an
old ram and tie it to a tree. Watch
how it breaks its horn and bruises
its head trying to get free. That
is what will happen to us again if
we fight Washington. Stay at home
and be at peace."[67]

Three years later, in 1871, Congress passed a law
declaring, in part, that no Indian Nation or tribe in
the territories of the United States would be recognized as an independent power with whom the
United States could sign a treaty. It also stated that
no former treaty with any Indian Nation or tribe
would be invalidated by this law.[68]

The Navajos could not comprehend the varied and
changing entities responsible for their welfare under
the system of reservation administration. The President, Congress , The Secretary of the Interior, The
Commissioner of Indian Affairs and all of the officials
were simply called "Washitone". The chief arbiter of
the fate of the Indians was and still is, Congress.
Congress was an unstable authority which represented a changing, growing nation where every group
was demanding a portion of the national funds. This
suited many citizens who were moving westward and
settling all over that area. The Navajos soon discovered that they lacked an informed and consistent
guardian with long-term plans for their welfare.
Their status remained that of the ward of a government that responded to political pressures more than
to their needs. Who can say what their future might
have been if the nation of the 1860's had possessed
an appreciation of the worthiness of minorities that it
possesses today.

The money promised to the Navajos by the treaty
was never fully appropriated by Congress. Every
year Congress authorized whatever amounts appeared
to be satisfactory or that they felt were affordable.

The Agent could do nothing about the shortage of funds except to complain to his superiors. In 1886, the Commissioner estimated that almost $800,000 was still owed the Navajos.

In addition to fiscal problems, there were droughts. In 1870 the harvested crops were insufficient, and in 1871 there were no crops at all. In 1873 the grain was gone by December causing a six month famine. In 1876 grasshoppers destroyed the grain crops and during the years of 1879 through 1881 there were more droughts. Most of the crops were spoiled by an early frost in 1882. There were more hunger-causing droughts for the next three years. Between 1900 and 1903 crops were poor and the people had to make do with insufficient rations. The rations were supplied by contractors in the east who often included such articles as suspenders, high-buttoned shoes, lead casters for furniture and other useless items.

The Agent was the only representative from Washington whom the Indians saw in the flesh. The Agent decided upon   the distribution of rations to those who were to receive special favors, and established the general rules of behavior on the reservation. His staff consisted of a clerk and sometimes an interpreter. The Agent was appointed by the Secretary of the Interior, usually as a political debt. But it was not easy to find a man, in or out of the party, who was willing to move thousands of miles to the west and live in substandard housing, isolated among Indians, for $1200 a year. The Agents came from the east and were usually appalled at what they found. Most of them left or were dismissed within a year or two. In the 33 years from 1869 to the end of the 19th century, there were 15 agents. Sometimes army officers filled in as temporary administrators.

Rations, seeds and tools could not surmount the difficulties caused by poor crops and unreliable weather. The Agents, regardless of their skills, could only report them to their superiors. Neither the agents nor Congress had the power or the interest to solve these problems.

Fumbling attempts were made at establishing inef-fective wind-mills, dams and ditches unsuited to the desert-like conditions. During this period of hardship the Navajos desperately tried to do their part to become self-sufficient. They were reported to be peaceful, well disposed, energetic, hardworking and industrious. [69]

During the 1870's the growing herds and increas-ing population made it difficult for the Navajos to live within the small area allotted to them.   Friction bet-ween the Navajos and non-Indians was increasing. Some Navajos began raiding the Zunis and ranchers. The old Headmen were called upon to stop these of-fenses.   Ganado Mucho and Manuelito determined that the raiders were involved in Navajo witchcraft and sent warriors to find and kill 40 suspected witches. One of those killed was Muerto de Hombre, a headman who signed the treaty. This action stopped all raiding and caused the witches to go underground.

During this period a cultural change took place on the reservation.   American traders followed in the footsteps of the Comancheros who traveled to these isolated areas in wagons loaded with trade goods, exchanging them for blankets, jewelry and   livestock. The American traders who brought outside products to the Navajos came to occupy a position of great importance in the Navajo way of life by building trading posts and living among the people. They provided a source to market reservation products. They were the only non-Indians who could communi-cate with the Navajo people in their own language and so became counselors, friends and confidants.

There have been cases of traders who were not trustworthy, cheating the Navajos in their dealings, but for the most part they served an important need. The trading posts still play an important role in the isolated areas of the reservation. In   recent years, some of these stores have been purchased and are now operated by Navajo traders.

By 1893 the old problems of increased livestock, soil erosion and reduced range feed produced a poorer and poorer quality of livestock. The Agent described the Navajos as being so poor that they could not even purchase the necessities of life.

The imprisonment of the Navajos in 1863 and 1864 brought about the first government directed search for captives. In the early months of 1864, General Carleton issued repeated orders for all Navajos to be sent to Bosque Redondo, including slaves. The New Mexicans ignored the orders. Garrison and post commanders throughout the territory carried out methodical investigations to determine who had Navajo slaves. The army searched the New Mexico settlements and found that the practice of owning slaves was so wide spread that it was almost impossible to carry out the orders. Many Navajos were recovered but there were those who no longer retained their native language, customs or habits. They were, in all respects, Mexican.

For several years after their return to their homeland from Fort Sumner the Navajos made a concerted effort to locate family members held in slavery. On several occasions during 1869 and 1870 Navajo headmen, with parents of children still in captivity, visited the Rio Grande settlements. Whenever they appealed directly to the New Mexicans, they were unsuccessful and were not even allowed to see or speak with the children. Agent Bennett liberated several children and returned them to their parents in 1870 and 1871. Every Agent for the next decade was faced with Indians seeking relatives held in slavery.

It was estimated that almost every New Mexican family had at least one Navajo slave and that many families had four or five. They traded them as they did their hogs and sheep. It was estimated that a minimum of 6,000 Navajos were held in slavery.[70] The effort to free the Navajos from slavery was never successful, and thousands grew up in that environment in Arizona, New Mexico and Texas.

The Spanish also held thousands of Puebloans in bondage serving as miners in Northern Mexico and as servants for individuals in other locations. They were an important part of the Spanish economy.

During the 1880's an effort was made to regain captives held by the Navajos. Many times when captives were freed by the Agents, they escaped and returned to the Navajos. Those who wished to return home were reunited with their families.

When given a choice, many captives chose to remain with the Navajos for they had married and had families. After their release from Fort Sumner, the Navajos no longer took slaves and the traditional practice of raiding ceased to exist.

Many people in the Rio Grande Valley have Navajo ancestors who were brought there through the slave system that flourished for so many centuries. There are many Navajos with Mexican and Puebloan ancestors from the early settlements along the Rio Grande River.

In 1875, New Mexican sheep men were grazing herds on the eastern boundary of the treaty reservation when the Atlantic and Pacific Railroad was granted alternate sections of land, 40-50 miles wide, on both sides of the right of way, creating a checker board pattern of ownership.

A delegation of headmen under the leadership of Manuelito went to Washington to plead with President Grant to save their grazing lands. The government offered them lands north of the San Juan River in exchange for the land lost to the railroads. The Headmen refused at first, but were convinced by the government officials to accept the trade.

A new system for expansion of the reservation developed. The numbers of livestock would increase, resulting in overgrazing of all of the grass lands. The Navajos would appeal to the government, and additions would be made to the reservation land to accommodate the increased livestock. This system was very successful until the reservation became hemmed in by other land owners. A workable system for stock reduction never was accepted by the Indians and the available lands again became depleted.

The largest reservation expansions were accomplished by executive orders of Presidents. Congress also approved additions in some areas. Both the government and the Navajo Tribe have purchased land to expand the reservation. In 1901 the government purchased the Mormon holdings in Tuba City, Arizona, for $48,000. In 1934 the first money in the amount of $481,879 was appropriated for the purchase of private land to add to the reservation.

In the 1950's the Navajo Tribe purchased the following lands: 1) the 100,000 acre Bar-N Ranch south of Sanders, Arizona, 2) the 76,618 acre Sergeant Ranch south of Crownpoint, New Mexico, and 3) a 56,000 acre area which the Navajos had leased from the Pueblos of Picuris and Pohoaque in New Mexico during the period of 1942-1956. This land was to be used by the Ramah Navajos. The latest purchase by the Navajo Tribe was the Boquillas Ranch of 491,000 acres for $33.4 million on July 6, 1987.

The Relocation Act of 1974 provided for the relocation of approximately 3,000 Navajos from joint use land belonging to the Hopis and 200 Hopis from joint use land that belonged to the Navajos. The government purchased 450,000 additional acres of private and public land for the use of relocated Navajos.

The Reservation does not appear crowded to the eyes of someone driving through it. One can travel for miles and never see a dwelling or any evidence of habitation. However, the Navajo population continues to grow at an unprecedented rate. Their birthrate is much higher than the national average. An increased life expectancy will cause the population to grow even more.

Productive land is limited, and employment oppor-tunities are rare. The grazing land for livestock is meager in most places. It is unlikely that the reser-vation land will be increased by any meaningful amount.

The majority of the Navajo population live in traditional or modified homes. As the population grows, the amount of land per capita will decrease. The time for individual land allotment has long passed. Many of the original allotments now belong to so many family members that no one uses the land. There are now too many people with too little good land to allot.

When President Arthur set aside this land for the joint-use of the Hopis and such other Indians as the government saw fit to settle there in 1882, he did not foresee the future problems of his decisions. It would appear that the President assumed, as did most Whites, that all Indians were the same and would get along together.

For hundreds of years there has been conflict between the Hopis and Navajos. These two tribes are very different. They neither speak the same language nor have similar life styles. The government always assumed that the two tribes could easily resolve their differences over this land. Finally, in 1974, Con-gress passed a law dividing the 2,500,000 acres of land almost equally between the two tribes.

The law contained a provision, to take place in 1976, for the government to reduce livestock in the joint-use area designated for Hopi use. Stock reduc-tion has always been a process that causes fear in

the Navajos.   The U.S. District Judge in Tucson,
Arizona, issued an injunction against moving the
livestock from the Hopi area until April of 1981.   The
Bureau of Indian Affairs began to reduce and im-
pound Navajo livestock on Hopi lands at that time.

However, after much publicity in the news media,
the Washington Office called a moratorium on the
reduction while they negotiated with the Navajo Tribe.
The Navajos filed a law suit in 1978 to prevent the
Department of the Interior from removing their livestock from the area awarded to the Hopis without an
Environmental Impact Statement.   This lawsuit was
dismissed by the U.S. District Judge in Phoenix,
Arizona on May 5, 1981.

The whole experience was summed up in the following statement:

> "The Bureau of Indian Affairs has
> had confrontations with the Navajo
> residents in an area called "Big
> Mountain".   The   opposition has been
> widely publicized and the American
> Indian Movement has become involved.
> This is a potentially dangerous situa-
> tion in that it can end in direct
> confrontation between the Navajos and
> the Hopis.
>
> The problem has not been handled
> well by the   political officials at the
> federal, state and tribal levels.   They
> have all, at one time or another, used
> this emotional situation to further
> their own political interests.
>
> The tragic aftermath is that even
> though different land has been set
> aside, with monies for the displaced
> Navajos, it is distant and not a part
> of their family or clan area.   It is not
> traditional Navajo land.   The families
> affected will undergo traumatic emo-

tional hardships to correct a problem
that should never have been allowed
to happen."[71]

MAP 6:   RESERVATION GROWTH

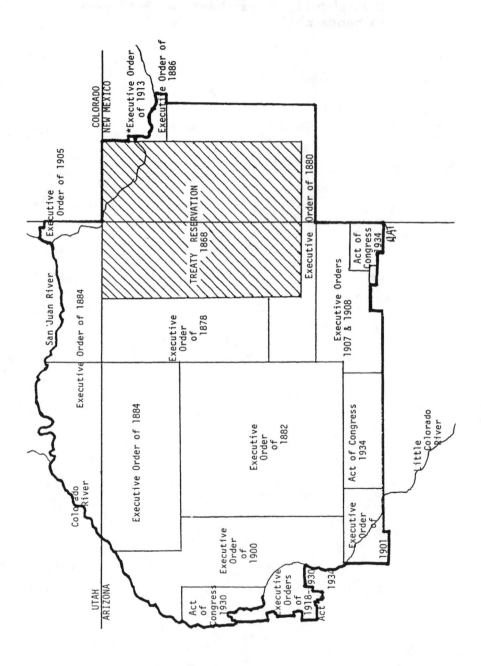

CHAPTER EIGHT

SELF-DETERMINATION

The Navajos were never a political entity. They were a group of people sharing a common language, culture and geographic region. Political organization did not extend beyond local bands led by headmen whose varying amounts of power were based upon their persuasive ability and not on hereditary authority. Coalitions of headmen were few and of short duration.

The first attempt on the part of the United States to form a government for the Navajos took place while they were in captivity at Fort Sumner. General Carleton planned to divide them into twelve villages with a principle chief to carry out the laws given to him for the government of the villages. Sub-chiefs would be appointed by the chief in the ratio of one for every hundred people and in the event of a vacancy in that office, the Commanding Officer would appoint a sub-chief to fill it. The Carleton plan failed to develop because the Navajos continued to live in the traditional manner.

Following the treaty of 1868, the Navajos continued without formal political organization. Between 1868 and 1901 Agents lived in Fort Defiance and had little contact with the other parts of the reservation. They leaned heavily upon former prominent headmen and sometimes called councils of those headmen. As the old leaders died off, Agents found it impossible to continue this practice.

After 1901 the reservation was gradually divided into six separate agencies which included the Hopis. Although there was a superintendent for each agency, it did nothing to foster the development of any tribal organization.

The superintendents selected for agencies were usually from the Land Operations Division of the Bureau of Indian Affairs.   A system of paternalisticly managed communities developed in which a reservation or agency superintendent directed the local form of government. Technicians planned projects such as irrigation, road construction, and education.   The superintendent then selected the projects to be approved, employing the workers and their supervisors without being answerable to those receiving the services.   He assigned newly developed lands and reassigned previously developed areas.   He hired and controlled the police who were paid with government funds.   He made the ultimate decision over Indian judges concerning punishment on the reservation.

The government planned and operated the school system without Indian participation. Government officials, far from the reservation, determined what the Indian problems were and how to solve them, using funds approved by Congress.   The only participation by Indians was that of being a recipient of the programs.

In 1921 oil was discovered on the treaty reservation and an oil company was authorized to negotiate with the Indians of the San Juan Agency. At a general meeting of the people in that agency, a development lease for 4,800 acres of land was approved. Soon after, three more leases were approved by a meeting of the people in the Southern Agency.   An additional lease was approved in the San Juan Agency but it was disallowed by the Secretary of the Interior.   He established a policy that gave the oil or gas to all members of the Navajo tribe and not just to the residents of a particular agency.   This policy forced attention to the   need   for   a   representative   tribal governing   body which   could act for all of the tribal members.

It is also indicative of the power of one person in government over the lives of many Indians. This policy, in effect, took away all land ownership from the Navajos, a policy still in effect to this day. All tribal actions concerning land must be approved by the Secretary of the Interior.

In 1923, the first version of a tribal council was established. The original membership consisted of one delegate and one alternate from each of the six agencies who elected a chairman and vice-chairman from among their members. This was changed to twelve delegates and twelve alternates in proportion to the population of each agency. The chairman was elected from candidates who were not council members while the vice-chairman was elected from the council by the delegates. Council meetings could be held only if called by the Commissioner of Indian Affairs. Henry Chee Dodge was elected as the first Tribal Council Chairman and served in this capacity until 1928. He had been appointed as Head Chief of the Navajo Tribe by an Agent after the death of the famous headman, Manuelito. He served in that role until his death in 1947. A new Head Chief has never been appointed.

In 1927, local community organizations called "Chapters" were formed. They were designed to bring local people together so that the Bureau of Indian Affairs officials could have better control. The Chapter movement spread throughout the reservation but temporarily stopped functioning during stock reduction. Chapters were revived in 1950, spreading to 96 communities throughout the reservation. For many years this form of government was much more influential than the artificially created Tribal Council.

In 1927, terms of office were changed from four years to five and provided contingencies for the death or removal of the chairman or vice-chairman. In 1928, women were allowed to vote, and the term of office was changed back to a four year period. These rules remained unchanged until 1934.

The early Council was criticized for not representing the people and was basically ignored until the stock reduction problems were referred to it. The

Bureau used this issue to empower the Council as the only official organization of the people. This action changed the attitude of the Navajos toward the power of the Council.[72]

The Navajo Tribe rejected the Indian Reorganization Act provisions by a vote of 7,992 to 7,608 in 1934. This would have allowed the Tribal Council to be organized along constitutional lines. The council then eliminated alternate delegates by declaring them delegates, thus doubling the size of the council. Perhaps the Navajos would have become independent many years sooner had they realized the benefits of the Indian Reorganization Act. It was argued by many government officials that they were not ready to govern themselves at that time. The original purpose for establishing the council was to approve oil and gas leases, but the organization was inadequate for the broad and pressing problems of the Navajo people.

In 1936 the Tribal Council called for a constitutional assembly to consider adopting a constitution or by-laws for the Navajo people. The Superintendent of the Navajo Agency was to select a 70 man Executive Committee from a list of 250 headmen that would represent all parts of the reservation.

The first meeting was held on the 9th and 10th of April, 1937. The assembled headmen argued over livestock and other problems and eventually made a motion to recognize the Constitutional Assembly as the Tribal Council, stating that it would develop a constitution and by-laws for the tribe. Henry Tallman was elected chairman and Roy Kinsel was elected vice-chairman. A proposed tribal constitution was presented to the Commissioner of Indian Affairs on October 25, 1937 but it was never approved by the Secretary of the Interior. Nevertheless, elections were held to replace the members of the Constitutional Committee who became the Tribal Council.

The Secretary approved the new Tribal Council,

declaring that it was his creation, and not an official
organization of the tribe empowered to exercise all of
the authority of such a body.   The Bureau of Indian
Affairs stated that this action would encourage the
tribe to develop a constitutional government that
would entitle it to the same powers and privileges as
other tribal governments under the Indian Reorganization Act.

The Secretary of the Interior developed the barest of
rules for governing the Tribal Council in 1938.   As a
creation of the Secretary, it could only exercise those
powers which he chose to recognize.   An election was
held on September 24, 1938 and the first official
meeting took place on November 8th.   Seventy-four
delegates were elected from areas within the land
management districts for a four year term.   The
executive heads of the Council were limited to two
terms in office.   The minimum voting age was established at 21.   Executive Committee members were
selected by fellow representative from each of the
land management districts.   Colors were used to identify candidates so that private ballots could be used.

The existing sovereign powers of Indian tribes are
those powers that Congress has not removed by law
or treaty.   Congress has allowed the tribes to retain
broad powers over its internal affairs and its natural
resources.   It has been generally accepted as a principle of law that the powers of self-government retained by Indian tribes originates with them as separate and sovereign nations who have treaties with the
United States.   If treaty provisions do not limit those
powers, then the laws of conquered nations can only
be changed by an enactment of law by the United
States Government.   The previous judicial decisions
were based upon three fundamental principles: 1)
an Indian tribe possessed all the powers of any
sovereign state,   2)   only conquest rendered the
tribe subject to the legislative powers of the United
States, terminating the external powers of the tribes
such as the power to enter into treaties with foreign
nations, but did not terminate the internal sovereign-

ty of the tribes allowing local self-government, and 3)
these internal powers could be modified by treaties or
by express legislation enacted by Congress.[73]

Many powers of internal sovereignty have remained with the Indian tribes and in their duly con-
stituted forms of government. Amendments and
changes in the Tribal Council's organization or
manner of election still requires Secretarial approval.

The United States Supreme Court has ruled that:

> "Originally the Indian tribes
> were separate nations within what is
> now the United States. Through
> conquest and treaties they were
> induced to give up complete inde-
> pendence and the right to war in
> exchange for federal protection, aid
> and grants of land. When the lands
> granted lay within the States, these
> governments sometimes sought to
> impose their laws and courts on the
> Indians.......
>
> Congress had consistently acted
> upon the assumption that the States
> have no power to regulate the affairs
> of Indians on a reservation. To
> assure adequate government of the
> Indian tribes it enacted comprehen-
> sive statutes in 1834 regulating
> trade with the Indians and organizing
> a Department of Indian Affairs.[74]

In 1950 the Secretary approved new procedures
for more effective representation; the use of picture
ballots, registration of voters, and the election of
Tribal Judges to office. In 1954 the responsibility for
elections was placed with the tribe and a Tribal Election Board. In 1959, the office of Tribal Judge was
changed to a lifetime appointment to be made by the
council with the approval of the Secretary of the

Interior.

Although the Council acted to consider a constitution, the draft was never submitted to the electorate.
There has never really been a demand on the part of
the Navajo people to change the present form of government.   As more and more people are educated and
become more civic minded they may some day act to
reorganize the governing body on a constitutional
basis.   The Navajo people do not consider the Council
as an instrument of the Secretary of the Interior, due
to the benign approval record of modern Secretaries.

The Navajo Tribal Council has always taken the
position that distribution of royalties and funds
received by the tribe to individuals would accomplish
little.   They have used the funds to finance programs
for the total tribal population, not individuals.   The
programs include but are not limited to :   scholar-
ships, community work programs, park systems, tourism, utility programs, arts and crafts development and
a police system.   The Tribe administers federal programs funded for states and cities as well as other
available programs they deem to be in the best interest of the Navajo people.

Two programs of the Navajo Tribal Council that
will have long lasting value to their people are the
tribal park service and the Chapter House/Community
Center construction programs. The Monument Valley
Navajo Tribal Park was established in 1950.   The Lake
Powell Navajo Tribal Park consisting of 2,218,112 acres
of land was established in 1962.   The Little Colorado
River Navajo Tribal Park was established that same
year.   Not only will the parks preserve areas of
natural beauty for future Americans, it will bring in
considerable amounts of revenue to the reservation
from tourism.

The Community Centers and Chapter Houses provide meeting places in even the most remote areas of
the reservation.   They provide a service that is not
offered by anyone else for the Navajo people in rural

areas.[75]

CHART 5: NAVAJO TRIBAL CHAIRMAN

Dates	Names
1923-1928	Chee Dodge
1929-1932	Deshna Chischillye
1933-1936	Thomas Dodge
1937-1938	Henry Tallman
1939-1942	Jacob C. Morgan
1943-1946	Chee Dodge
1947-1954	Sam Ahkeah
1955-1962	Paul Jones
1963-1970	Raymond Nakai
1971-1982	Peter MacDonald
1983-1986	Petersen Zah
1987-1989 Suspended	Peter MacDonald
1990-Present	Petersen Zah

   The whole concept of the sovereignty of a reservation has come under close scrutiny by states containing large sections of reservation lands.   For
example, the lack of sufficient funds to operate
reservation based public schools has long been a
concern to the state of Arizona.   The most recent test
of sovereignty for all Indians on reservations has
been over gambling.   This is a new source of revenue
from bingo palaces and casinos with slot machines and

card games. The Navajos have not expressed interest as yet, but if other tribes in Arizona are successful, it will only be a matter of time before they enter the gambling game.

The Navajo Tribal Council continues to operate without a constitution. There have been discussions recently of enacting a constitution, but until such time as there is a demonstrated need, things will continue as they have in the past.

On the reservation, state government entities exist side by side with tribal and federal programs. The highways are maintained and patrolled by the state and tribal police. Public schools operate within the laws of the states in which they are located, with school boards whose elected officials are predominantly Navajo. A public school board member is the only elected office that can be filled by a non-Navajo on the reservation. State welfare and social programs operate on the reservation, usually manned by Navajo employees. State and federal elections are conducted on the reservation under the same rules as elsewhere.

The Navajo Tribal Council enacted legislation in 1977 that would have taxed all of the utility companies operating on the Navajo reservation and the millions of tons of coal removed from the reservation. This decision was challenged in the courts. The Court of Appeals ruled in favor of the companies in 1981, but higher courts reaffirmed Indian sovereignty.

Considering that Indians were not recognized as citizens until 1924, and that they could not vote in state and national elections in New Mexico and Arizona until 1949, their political activity and growth has been phenomenal. In 1964 James Atcitty and Monroe Jymm were elected to the House of Representatives in the State of New Mexico. In 1966 Lloyd House was elected to the House of Representatives in Arizona and Tom Lee was elected to the state Senate in New Mexico. In 1972 Arthur Hubbard was elected to the state Senate of Arizona, the first Navajo to serve in this capacity.   Senator Hubbard served six terms in that office.   Daniel Peaches and Benjamin Hanley have served in the House of Representatives in Arizona. Representative Hanley and Senator Hubbard served as "long ears" or Democrats.   Representative Peaches served as "roper with his nose" or Republican.

Navajo Senators and Representatives continue to serve in the Arizona and New Mexico State Legis-latures representing their political regions.   In Arizo-na, Navajos are also serving on Boards of Supervisors in Apache, Navajo and Coconino Counties.   However, non-Indians may not serve on the Tribal Council, causing conflicting political pressures.

It is particularly difficult for the state to accept the idea of a treaty with a group of people who enjoy all the privileges of citizenship with no responsibility to pay for it.   The fact that Navajo land is exempt from state control and taxes, and the lack of non-Indian participation in tribal government, while Nava-jos hold county and state offices, is creating an ongoing debate that will probably end up in Con-gress, or in the hands of the Supreme Court.

In Arizona, legislation was introduced in 1977 and again in 1981 to establish a large portion of the Navajo reservation as a separate county.   The Navajo Tribal Chairman and Navajo legislators averted the passage of the bill by making certain concessions to the state.

In 1981 legislation was introduced to redraw the boundaries of two counties that lay within the Navajo reservation.   It was proposed that the northern sec-tions of the two counties would become Navajo Coun-ty.   Southern Apache County would retain its identi-ty, but the southern portion of Navajo County would be known as Holbrook County or Hopi County.   The legislation was shelved and a special legislative committee was appointed to study the problem after Governor Bruce Babbitt vetoed the bill.   The issue received wide attention in the state and one newspaper explained the situation in this way:

> "Apache County-They do things in their own way in the great expanse of Apache County. Tucked away in the northeast corner of Arizona-home of the Painted Desert and the Petrified Forest-the high plateau "cattle country" has always written its own rules.
> So that's why it ignored three-fourths of its own population-every Indian living on its gigantic Navajo Reservation in the northern section of the county-when it drew new district lines for the Board of Supervisors in 1972.

> That's why it went to court to stop the U.S. Justice Department from imposing districts that assure one-person-one vote.

> That's why it tried to prevent the first Indians ever elected to the Board of Supervisors from holding office.

> That's why it wants its county split in two, ridding it of the 34,300 Navajos who not only hold the majority status in population, but have a majority of seats on the county's governing board.

> This year, for the first time in six tries, the Arizona Legislature accepted cries of "taxation without representation" and passed a bill to sever the reservation, creating the state's 15th county composed entirely of Indians. Blasting the bill as "segregationist", Democratic

> Governor Bruce Babbitt vetoed it.
> And then to the amazement of many,
> the Republican-dominated Legislature
> couldn't muster enough votes to over-
> ride his rejection.
>
> But that isn't the end of the
> controversy. A similar bill undoubt-
> edly will show up at the Statehouse
> next year. Because they write their
> own rules in Apache County, and this
> rule burns deepest."[76]

The "New Times" goes on to explain why Indians
who live on reservations don't pay property taxes. It
quotes Supervisor Louise Dennison:

> "It is not my decision as one Navajo
> to pay property taxes. That decision
> belongs to the U. S. Congress-not me.
> It was the Treaty of 1868 that de-
> clared Indian property would not be
> taxed. And when Arizona wanted to
> become a state, it included the same
> clause in its constitution. Besides, I
> don't own the land. The U. S.
> Government holds it in trust for my
> people. We get permission from the
> federal government to build a home,
> put livestock on it, run a business."[77]

The financial and social conditions that are changing for the nation and the world will have an impact
on the Navajos of the southwest. Power generators
that burn coal mined on the reservation are now
being built off reservation because companies fear
poor judgment by the Navajo Tribal Council in taxing
their operations. This will eliminate many highly paid
jobs on the reservation. It is doubtful that the
taxation would adequately recompense the Navajo
workers for the loss of these jobs. When the American Indian Movement took over an electronics factory
in Shiprock, New Mexico, the company closed down

operations, causing some 500 Navajos to lose jobs, and moved to a city where they would have adequate police protection.

Navajo leaders will have to develop skills in dealing with industry that differ from those skills used in dealing with the Bureau of Indian Affairs and other governmental agencies. Industry will not operate in an arena of confrontation. It will require patience and effort on the part of those wishing successful interaction.

The Navajo Tribal Council will be hard pressed to deal with the external pressures it will feel in the very near future. The actions taken in far off Window Rock will now have direct impact upon non-Indian people living in the fast growing cities of the southwest.

The abundant coal, water and oil resources will impact upon the growth of these cities for many generations, and will be a viable source of income to the Indians as long as their costs are not so high that they drive businesses to seek other sources. This concern is now being put to the test.

On April 26, 1989, the U. S. Supreme Court ruled that the state of New Mexico had the right to levy state taxes against Cotton Petroleum Inc., which extracts oil and natural gas from the Jicarilla Apache Reservation. There are 150 similar cases pending in Arizona, New Mexico, Montana, and Utah by energy companies who see themselves as victims of illegal multiple taxation by states and tribes. One energy representative states that, "Tribes around the country will have trouble attracting businesses to reservations because of double taxation." Duane Beyal, spokesperson for the Navajo Tribe stated: "This specter of double taxation has always been a huge objection from the companies we do business with."[78]

The Navajo Tribe will now have to evaluate this revenue. If it reduces the tax, the result will be less

revenue. If it is repealed, the result will be a total
loss of revenue. To continue taxation will hamper
future employment and business development.   The
final confrontation will be in Congress, if the Tribal
Council does not act in a judicious and careful
manner in the coming years.

This fact has not escaped the attention of the
news media. A Phoenix newspaper carried the following information about the problems of the Indians in
Arizona. Peter MacDonald, Navajo Tribal Chairman in
the late 1960's and 1970's, said:

> "There was an Indian awakening, a
> renaissance. We began to take charge
> of our lives-reintroduced our native
> languages, returned more of our
> culture to our children's education,
> and strengthened our political base.
>
> Now, we're back to the 1860's--a
> complete circle. The government
> wants our land. Others are trying to
> get our energy resources. Still more
> want our water.   Others won't recog-
> nize our laws. We're in a different
> kind of confrontation--in courts, in
> state legislatures, in Washington.
>
> But this time we will win."[79]

The confrontation between Indians and others has
been confirmed by various government officials, tribal
and non-tribal lawyers, congressional staff members,
university representatives, tribal representatives, and
similar experts. The six major areas of opposition
plaguing the Navajos concern water, energy, Indian
taxing power, the political process, interaction between tribal and local governments and federal funding.

Chairman MacDonald was defeated in 1982 by
Peterson Zah. The Navajo people felt that they wanted

a change and a younger outlook on the problems.
To his credit, Zah took a less militant approach to the
Navajo-Hopi land problems. He met with Chairman
Ivan Sidney of the Hopi Tribe several times to defuse
some of the tensions of the time. They had attended
school together and were able to communicate well
with each other, yet in the final analysis, nothing
was settled. Chairman Zah built up the depleted
reserve funds of the Navajo Tribe from 30 million
dollars when he took over to 100 million dollars when
he left office. He was considered frugal with funds.
A master plan for urban development was developed
under his leadership based upon the selection of ten
population centers on the reservation. He initiated
the development of a shopping center and an urban
infrastructure around federal agencies in Kayenta,
which will soon have its own town council.[80]

Zah was defeated by MacDonald again in 1987 after
one term in office. The return of MacDonald to the
Chairman's office was fraught with strife and recrimi-
nation, but he reestablished his office and began
operations.

In 1988 the Arizona Republic, a newspaper in
Phoenix, Arizona, ran a series of articles called
"Fraud in Indian Country." These   dealt with allega-
tions of fraud and mismanagement of the federal
government's trust responsibility for Indian people,
their lands and their resources. It appeared that, in
some cases, oil companies were taking more oil than
they were paying for, cheating Indians out of millions
of dollars over a period of years. The wide interest
in this series caused the Senate to establish a Special
Select Committee on Indian Affairs. Senator Daniel
Inouye, D-Hawaii, was selected as chairman. Senator
DeConcini and Senator McCain of Arizona were appointed co-chairmen of the Special Committee on
Investigations.   The committee conducted public
hearings and investigated many Indian tribes, not
just the Navajo, for a variety of reported problems.

The committee heard testimony that Chairman

MacDonald allegedly committed acts that were possibly criminal in nature or at the least, examples of bad judgment, such as spending $650,000 to remodel his office, paying $20,000 for a private jet trip for his family, spending $1,500,000 on public relations and lobbying with the Madison Public Affairs Group in Washington, D.C.[81] The chairman was also accused of seeking a $45,000 kick-back from an aircraft broker, and enabling the tribe to purchase the 491,000 acre Boquillas Ranch for $33.4 million from two life-long friends. Tenneco, Inc. said they would have sold the ranch for 17.8 million.[82]

The early conclusions from the hearings were most interesting and show some understanding of the problems: Tribal officials are not the traditional tribal leaders of the past, but preside over tribal governments, which are sovereign bodies. These leaders are duly elected public officials. Their budgets are supported not only by their own revenues, but also by federal revenues. They must be made accountable for these funds by the same standards which the federal government applies to non-Indian officials.

These leaders have been denied the respect and authority that go with their position. Instead of being consulted and included in the rule-making and regulation process, as are other elected officials, Indian elected representatives often have been denied a voice in the policies affecting their lives by officials who are, in some cases, ignorant or unwilling to acknowledge the Indian leader's status. Those who seek illicit gain from funds and programs intended for the benefit of Indian people should be subject to harsh penalties, whether they be a federal government employee, a private company official or a tribal leader.

The committee presented comprehensive recommendations to address the many facets of the problem, both in and out of the government. They included these specific actions: a gradual elimination of the BIA, the creation and funding of the Office of

Federal-Tribal Relations as a part of the executive branch, and direct revenue sharing with tribes to create their own programs.   To receive these monies the tribes would have to meet strict accounting procedures and adopt a constitutional form of government with separate administrative, judicial and executive branches.[83] A general consensus of opinion seems to be that while the tribe would receive funds to run things their way, Congress would likely set its own agenda by controlling the funds.

The committee's report has not brought the wide acceptance that it appeared to have in the early stages of its operation.   Critics accuse the investigation of being more like entertainment than a platform for reform.   P. Sam Deloria, director of the American Indian Law Center at the University of New Mexico in Albuquerque made several observations.

> "The inconsistencies of the report is astonishing," Deloria said. "For example, while on one hand the report said tribes should have greater freedom, it also said that both the U.S. Attorney's Office and the FBI should beef up its operations on Indian reservations."

> "That really means moving from the Bureau of Indian Affairs of old to the paternalism of the U.S. Attorney's, administering tribes through the criminal laws," Deloria said.

> "Tribes do not have the power to prosecute felonies on the reservation. MacDonald, for example, is charged with 107 misdemeanor counts."[84]

Peter MacDonald was sentenced to a seven-year term in the tribal jail for bribery, conspiracy, fraud and extortion.   In November, 1992, he was convicted of conspiracy and assault-related charges stemming from a riot on July 20, 1989, when nearly 200 MacDon-

ald supporters attacked police officers and stormed
the tribe's administration building.   On February 17,
1993, he was sentenced by Judge Robert Broomfield of
the U. S. District Court in Phoenix to a fourteen and
one half year jail term for conspiracy and burglary
and fined $5,000.   It is to be served concurrently
with the seven year sentence.[85]

    Perhaps something positive can come from all this
adversity.   It is possible that the Navajo people and
the BIA will realize that the time has come to formu-
late a constitution, to develop self-determination, and
to utilize the advantages that will accompany these
actions.

CHAPTER NINE

A CLASSROOM FOR EVERY THIRTY CHILDREN

ARTICLE VI.

"In order to insure the civilization of the Indians entering into this treaty, the necessity of education is admitted, especially of such of them as may be settled on said agricultural parts of this reservation, and they therefore pledge themselves to compel their children, male and female, between the ages of six and sixteen years, to attend school; and it is hereby made the duty of the agent for said Indians to see that this stipulation is strictly complied with; and the United States agrees that, for every thirty children between said ages who can be induced or compelled to attend school, a house shall be provided, and a teacher competent to teach the elementary branches of an English education shall be furnished, who will reside among said Indians, and faithfully discharge his or her duties as a teacher.

The provisions of this article to continue for not less than ten years.[86]

The purpose of early Indian education programs was to prepare children to enter the white society by removing them from their home influences and transporting them far away in order to eliminate their native culture.

Although 95 percent of the children returned home after finishing school, no effort was made to prepare them for the existing reservation conditions, creating a disadvantage because they did not know the customs of their own people. At school, the children were forbidden to speak their own language, and a military-like discipline was practiced. Pupils spent their childhood in a system which could not offer the benefits of family life comparable even to the poorest of Indian homes. The traditional and educational system of the white man did not meet the needs of the Navajo people. The traditional Navajo society provided educational experiences at home designed to teach the fundamentals of agriculture and stock raising, the legends, the taboos and the practices of Navajo religion. The ability to read and write a foreign language and to learn to live like a foreigner did not make any sense to the Navajo people.

When the Navajos returned from Fort Sumner there were no schools to educate their children so the government turned to the churches and their mission boards for assistance. The Department of Interior agreed to furnish a schoolhouse and to pay the missionary teacher $600 a year. The first teacher was sent by the Presbyterian Home Mission to Fort Defiance. The young teacher, coming from the east, must have been dismayed at what she found.

Many Navajos lived nearby and those who had no work for their children sent them to school. Many felt that if their children were to be killed by the white man's magic, they would suffer a minimal loss if they sent the sickly ones. Even then, they were sent for only a day or two each month. Some days there were three children, on others thirty-three, but rarely the same children. At the end of the term, the teacher married and left to work with more civilized Indians. In 1872, the school was reported as useless due to the irregular attendance of students.[87]

One Agent brought weavers and looms to teach

students modern weaving methods but the project was a total failure. The Navajos already had traditional methods of weaving that they would not change. Teachers came and went from the Home Mission Board, sometimes all leaving together.

By 1879, Congress was persuaded by the Bureau of Indian Affairs to authorize a boarding school at Fort Defiance. Even though Congress agreed with the need for a school they did not authorize any funds for its construction the first year. The second year $875 was appropriated. Funds continued to dribble in and it took two more years to finally complete the buildings. More teachers were hired, separate dormitories for boys and girls were completed, desks were installed in classrooms, a kitchen, a laundry and a dining room were equipped. In 1884, 22 students were in attendance and by November there were 24. The next year, with the help of the police, the enrollment increased to 33 students.

In 1887, Congress passed the Compulsory Indian Education Law. The ten year period of providing education called for in the treaty had long passed without ever becoming a 'reality. Now Congress decided that the education and civilization of the Indian youth of America was its concern and passed a law to enforce the process. Thereafter the Navajo educational program developed some of the appearances of a penal system. Pupils were, in every sense, prisoners and discipline was enforced with the same harshness exercised in penal institutions. Agents, accompanied by police, forcefully took children from their homes and transported them to boarding schools. Many were taken to government schools outside of their sacred lands, into New Mexico, Colorado, Nevada, Arizona and as far away as Pennsylvania.

Eventually some schools were established at agency headquarters in Tuba City, Leupp , Tohatchi, Shiprock, Toadalena and Fort Wingate. The educa-

ILLUSTRATION 6:   STUDENTS AND WORKERS AT
FORT DEFIANCE BEFORE 1894.

Source: Underhill, Ruth., *Here Come the Navajo*, Lawrence: Haskell Institute Press, 1953. 216.

Bureau of American Ethnology

tional programs from 1869 to 1897 was almost totally in the hands of the mission groups. The Presbyterians, Methodists, Catholics and the Christian Reformed Church received federal subsidies.

There are those who feel that the opening of the reservation schools to missionary organizations was one of the greater injuries inflicted upon the Navajos by the federal government. Religious zealots were given permission by the government to force their beliefs upon captive Indian school children by what ever intellectual or physical means they chose. Many Navajos suffered an emotional trauma from which they never recovered.[88]   Schools are still operated by Mission groups on the reservation and their primary purpose is still to convert children to their religious beliefs, but the children who attend these schools now do so freely and with the encouragement and support of their parents and relatives.

In 1897, Congress decided that it should provide the education of Indian children and declared that sectarian schools could no longer receive government appropriations. Mission Boards brought their influence to bear to obtain money from treaty and tribal resources and received those funds from the Bureau of Indian Affairs until 1917.

A statute was enacted that year that prohibited any appropriation from the Treasury of the United States to be used for the education of Indian children in any sectarian school. Although no federal funds were available to them, the mission schools continued to grow for the next 30 years. The Mormons, Mennonites, Seventh Day Adventists, Navajo Gospel Crusade, Church of the Brethren, Quakers, Plymouth Brethren, Global Gospel Fellowship, and the Navajo Bible Academy opened schools in Utah, Colorado, New Mexico and Arizona.

The schools for the Navajos, from the beginning at Fort Defiance to the middle of the 20th century, retained the goal of eliminating Navajo culture. They

operated under the philosophy that if these children
were to be fit to enter the white society, they must
be removed from their environment and prevented
from having contact with families for at least four,
and preferably six to eight years. During that time,
they would not be allowed to speak their native
tongue and were intermingled with tribes that did not
speak Navajo so that they would have to speak English to communicate with their classmates. In order
to drive the heathen teachings from their minds the
children were required to wear the clothing of the
white child, forbidden to play any Navajo games, and
in effect, were to become white children. They were
taught to labor, to assume responsibilities, and were
disciplined when they broke the rules in order to
teach them the correct behavior of civilized people.
Nothing that would remind them of their homes,
parents or their world was to enter their lives. The
ways of the Navajos had to be forever lost to these
children so that they would never want to return.

Dormitories, kitchens, farms, and canneries were
manned by untrained and unskilled personnel who did
not know how to deal with children. They were given
the freedom by the professional personnel to deal
with problems as they saw fit. Indian adults have
reported terrible stories of their school experiences
under that philosophy. One woman recalled that she
was whipped because she could not sing a song in
front of a group of students. Because she did not
want to cry publicly, she was whipped until she did
cry. She also reported that the cooks whipped the
children who worked in the kitchens and in one
instance a boy was beaten unconscious by an employee. Demerits were given and were worked off
by standing while eating, standing on a stool while
everyone else ate or by standing outside in the hot
afternoon sun from one to five o'clock on Sunday
afternoons. One form of punishment required students to carry heavy logs on their shoulders around
the playground in the evenings and on weekends.
There are recorded instances where students ran
away, only to freeze to death or to lose hands and

feet in the snow and cold, trying to reach their homes. Students were picked up in wagons while herding sheep and sent off to schools for four or five years before being taken back and released in the same general area. Parents did not know what had happened to them during that period and in some instances assumed that they were dead.

In 1927, the government authorized a special committee, headed by Louis Merriam, under the direction of the Institute of Governmental Research, to submit a report that could be used as a guide to enact progressive programs and to determine the funds needed to ease the educational conditions of the Navajos.

In June of 1928, Merriam issued a report that shocked the nation. In his report he stated that his committee had spent almost two years visiting Indian schools to observe reservation facilities and found the following conditions: pupils, when given an opportunity to play, merely sat and stared at the ground; schools were forced to produce their own food due to the lack of appropriations; the schools used the term "vocational education" to describe practically enslaved pupils who worked on farms, ran dairies, repaired shoes, and laundered clothing; cleaning tasks were performed under strict discipline; the children were forced to maintain a pathetic quietness and could not even have conversations in the dining hall; when dairies had milking machines, youngsters were forced to milk by hand, rising early and working late for the entire year; there was never enough space for beds and students slept on attic floors or two to a bed in cramped quarters; children, even small ones, worked in the laundry in overcrowded rooms filled with steam; the children who were doing all of the work were found by competent medical personnel to be malnourished; eleven and twelve year old children were spending four hours a day in heavy industrial work in most schools; discipline practices were as harsh as those used in a reform school; these deplorable conditions were caused by the reluctance of the U. S. Congress to adequately fund the schools; and

the incompetent teachers and administrators meted
out excessively harsh punishment in their ignorance.
The wave of public indignation caused by this report
forced Congress to do something about the Navajo
educational practices of the 1930's.[89]

By 1936, The Bureau of Indian Affairs had opened
numerous day schools in areas of heaviest population
so that pupils could live at home and be bused to
and from school. Parents could keep in touch with
the educational process and assure themselves that
their children were being treated properly while
learning about the community schools.

The day school movement was doomed to failure
from the start because the government failed to
provide funds for road improvement that would allow
buses to pick up children. Only those schools in
areas where pupils were within walking distance or
could come in on horseback continued to operate.
The others were closed or converted to boarding
schools. With the outbreak of World War II, road
work ceased when funds were cut and the buses
were discontinued.

The problems of operating reservation schools
were compounded by wartime shortages and restrictions. Appropriations were totally inadequate. Many
of the day schools were converted to makeshift boarding schools with Quonset hut dormitories. Some
children were crowded into chapter houses and
unsuitable buildings with no utilities other than a
wood burning stove. In more than one area parents
built dormitories with their own hands, so that
their children could go to school near home.
Navajo parents were willing to make great sacrifices
during these years to assure the education of their
children. In some schools, dormitory attendants and
cooks became teachers.

When Navajo servicemen and war workers returned to the reservation after World War II, they
realized that isolation from the outside world was no

ILLUSTRATION 7:   STUDENTS AT SHIPROCK SCHOOL

Source: Underhill, Ruth., *Here Come the Navajo*, Lawrence: Haskell Institute Press, 1953. 230.

Jacob Morgan

longer possible.   They had become too dependent
upon outside goods and materials.   A special tribal
delegation advised the Secretary of the Interior that
education was the single greatest need of the tribe.
School facilities were needed for the children of some
70,000 citizens of the United States who were growing
up illiterate and unable to speak the national language.

In March of 1948, the Secretary of the Interior
submitted a report, with elements of many previous
reports. An appropriation of 90 million dollars was
approved to finance a long-range program designed
to help the Navajo adjust to the new conditions of
living, and to reach parity with their fellow citizens.
An early bill was vetoed by President Truman because
an added amendment violated the principle of tribal
self-determination and passed power over Indian
water rights to the state courts. Truman felt that this
plan would provide less   protection of Indian water
rights.

The bill passed in the spring of 1950 and was
signed by the President.   The program contained the
following provisions:

Number	Amount	Purpose
1)	$10,000,000	Soil and water conservation
2)	$500,000	Surveys and studies
3)	$1,000,000	Industrial development
4)	$3,500,000	Off-reservation employment and resettlement
5)	$5,750,000	Relocation and resettlement of Navajos along the Colorado River
6)	$20,000,000	Roads and trails

7)	$250,000	Communications
8)	$2,500,000	Domestic and institutional water development
9)	$5,000,000	Credit
10)	$4,750,000	Health services
11)	$25,000,000	Education
12)	the remainder	Housing and common services[90]

In 1952 and 1953 $6,448,000 was appropriated for school construction, adding approximately 250 school seats and standard dormitories to replace dangerous makeshift facilities. Half of the children of school age remained out of school because accommodations were not available or were inadequate. Many schools also suffered with poor water supplies, poor phone systems, and little or no electricity.

In 1954, the Tribal Council adopted a resolution authorizing the Commissioner to take whatever steps might be necessary to accomplish the objective of universal education for the youth of the tribe, and the Navajo Emergency Education Program was born. The immediate objective was to provide seats for an additional 7,946 Navajo children by September and to raise enrollment to a minimum of 22,052.

The 1954 appropriation of $6,171,000 was programmed to: make better use of existing space in old facilities; place trailer schools in strategic locations; build dormitories in border towns to house those going to public schools; construct new schools and additions to old schools; construct new dormitories, housing and other necessary facilities. See Appendix D for history of school construction.

The Tribal Council provided $350,000 for the purchase of children's clothing as an incentive to in-

crease school enrollment and to meet the actual needs
of many families. In 1955 the Commissioner of Indian
Affairs published a policy for general education that
had been approved by the Navajo Tribe. The government was committed: to develop educational opportunities on the reservation for grades beginner
through six, allowing the younger children to be
closer to their parents during their formative years;
to develop educational opportunities in the public
schools for junior and senior high levels; and to
continue the Special Navajo Education Program to
combine vocational and academic education adapted to
the special needs of children 13-18 years old, two or
more years below grade level, or who had not previously been to school.[91]

The 1950's were a time of great excitement and
activity on the Navajo Reservation. School construction activities in all parts of the reservation provided
new employment opportunities. Hundreds of jobs
became available in the schools for dormitory attendants, cooks, janitors, maintenance men, and bus driv-
ers. Trailer schools were being located in isolated
areas. Small International four-wheel drive school
buses made the rounds on wagon roads to pick up
school children each morning. Schools that had been
closed during World War II were reopened. Hundreds
of new teachers arrived from all over the United
States, bringing the vitality of excellently trained
professionals to the schools. There were new dark
faces among the teaching ranks as Afro-Americans
began working for the government in large numbers.
Many of the small schools in isolated areas were
manned by husband and wife teams and the comra-
deship between the teachers and other school employees was very warm and real. They exchanged
ideas and discussed the problems of keeping these
small schools open to educate the young students in
their communities.

The employees of off-reservation boarding schools
visited the homes of Navajo students to recruit other
students to fill their projected enrollments in special

programs in Oregon, California, Utah, Arizona, Nevada, New Mexico and Oklahoma. In August, the night skies were brightened by the fires of Squaw Dances being held to protect the students from danger while they journeyed far from their sacred lands. Greyhound and Trailway buses traveled into remote parts of the reservation to transport thousands of students to those far away boarding schools. Now they were going with their parents' blessings and permission. The buses returned in May bringing laughing boys and girls home to their anxiously awaiting parents and relatives. The government made an effort to bring education to the Navajo with a vigor that was unparalleled in history, as depicted in Chart 5.

CHART 5: ENROLLMENT FOR THE TEN-YEAR PERIOD 1950-1960

TYPE OF SCHOOL	1950	1960	DIFFERENCES
BOARDING SCHOOLS:			
RESERVATION:	7,340	10,000	2,660
NON-RESERVATION:	2,041	5,408	3,367
DAY SCHOOLS:			
REGULAR:	742	931	189
TRAILER:		541	541
PUBLIC SCHOOLS:			
RESERVATION:	1,837	7,430	5,593
BORDERTOWN DORMITORIES:		3,134	3,134
MISSION AND OTHER:	1,175	1,379	204
TOTAL ENROLLMENT: AGES 6-18	13,135	28,824	15,689
TOTAL ENROLLMENT: AGES UNDER 6 AND OVER 18	748	1,826	1,078
TOTAL ALL STUDENTS:	13,883	30,650	16,767[92]

Navajo children entered reservation boarding schools without speaking the English language. Their first year was spent in learning to speak English in the classroom and learning about non-Indian culture. Entering the first grade at the age of seven automatically placed a child one full grade behind his counterpart in off-reservation public schools. Many parents still did not enroll their children in school when they were six and others attended irregularly.

The individual ability of a student to learn English, the intensity of acculturation in his home and other allied factors caused most Navajo children to test much lower than other students in the nation. Public schools now accept students at age five in kindergarten. The Navajo Tribal Headstart Program provides a good pre-school program so that the Navajo child is chronologically in step with the rest of the nation.

A more coordinated effort on the part of different entities responsible for the education of Navajo students, to evaluate their goals of education, has become critical. Each school system goes its own way and may or may not have similar goals and programs.

Hildegarde Thompson, former BIA administrator, said that when the needs of the Indian become the same as for the non-Indian, then:

> "Indians will choose from available sources that which they see as useful in their lives. The acceptance of newer and useful aspects of contemporary life will often require a change in attitude and thinking. Most likely, it will mean the development of new skills and a reinterpretation of values in relationship to the newer conditions Indians face.
> When the choices are made by the Indians themselves, new concepts will be properly related to the

old concepts and both integrated in
such a way that they will become
an accepted part of Indian
thinking."[93]

The Navajo Tribal Government has invested millions of dollars and uses the interest for a Navajo
Education Scholarship Fund. The money is used to
provide free grants to promising young men and
women who want to attend colleges and universities.
It also operates the federal Head Start Program for
pre-school children.

The latest figures available indicate that over 90
percent of the students living on the reservation are
attending schools of their choice. But no matter how
many school opportunities are available, some Navajo
children will be brought up in the traditional ways in
the remote areas of the reservation. It seems inevitable that brothers and sisters will take turns going
to school only when they are not needed at home to
tend sheep or to baby-sit. For all practical purposes, the Navajo child of today can attend a school of
his choosing, whether it be public, Bureau of Indian
Affairs or Mission, and in some instances tribal
schools. Article VI of the treaty promising a classroom and a teacher for every 30 children has become
a reality.

CHAPTER TEN

CONTINUING PROBLEMS OF EDUCATION

The words of Manuelito, a famous Headman, spoken to Chee Dodge after returning from Fort Sumner, are as meaningful today as they were when he said:

> "My grandchildren, the Whites have many things we Navajos need. But we cannot get them. It is as though the Whites were in a grassy canyon and there they have wagons, plows, and plenty of food. We Navajos are up on a dry mesa.
>
> We can hear them talking but we cannot get to them. My Grandchildren, education is the ladder. Tell our people to take it."[94]

One major continuing problem of education concerns who is going to govern the schools on the Navajo reservation. A conflict developed between public and bureau schools on the reservation in the 1960's. As new paved roads were developed in different parts of the reservation, public school buses were requested by parents so that their children could be at home with them. The bureau lost more students when the Mormon Church began a program to provide foster homes for Navajo children with members of their church, in off-reservation cities, so that students could attend public schools. The bureau constructed two new high schools, one at Many Farms and one at Tuba City. The Navajo Community College shared the campus at Many Farms High School. When the college moved to its permanent campus at Tsaile, so many rooms were left vacant that the whole bureau school population was moved to Many Farms from

Chinle in the 1970's. The high school at Tuba City merged with the public high school in 1972, becoming an amalgamated high school, but the merger was dissolved when controversy developed over the authority of the Navajo Tribe in public schools.

Many students live with relatives along the public school bus routes on the Navajo Reservation. Others walk many miles to the highway to catch a bus, even in very cold weather. Some public school bus routes are from 50-75 miles long, one way. Even now, many inhabited areas of the reservation do not have improved roads, compelling students living there to attend boarding schools until such time as buses become available to them. Public schools continue to grow in enrollment and programs as funds are available.

In the mid-1960's, the needs of the public schools became so great that large numbers of portable facilities were provided for classrooms, and trailer houses were purchased for living quarters for teachers. Increases in Federal funding allowed the BIA to build decidedly modern houses instead of apartments, and to provide such niceties as ceramic wainscoting in school hallways.

A shift of Navajo students to public and mission schools continued to overcrowd these facilities, leaving the Bureau schools with vacant classrooms, and yet the BIA continued to upgrade and replace existing facilities. Funding requests were made in 1987 in these areas: Tuba City Elementary School and Headquarters, Beclabito Day School, Crystal Boarding School, Wide Ruins Boarding School, Low Mountain Boarding School, Low Mountain Sewer Lagoons, Shonto Boarding School, Nazlini Boarding School, Tuba City High School, and Rough Rock Demonstration School.[95]

Two new public school districts were formed on

the reservation by dividing larger districts. Keams
Canyon Public School District existed on the Hopi
Reservation for many years. Its boundaries extended
onto the Navajo Reservation and some Navajo students
attended. The public school district could obtain
neither land nor buildings from the BIA or from the
Hopi Tribe in order to expand. High school students
who wanted to stay with their families had to ride a
bus provided by the public school to Holbrook, Arizona, some 78 miles one way. Students did this for
years, leaving before sunup and coming home in the
dark. When a high school was built at Ganado,
students were bused 50 miles one way.

Then, in the early 1980's, Cedar Unified School
District No. 25 was formed from the old Keams Canyon
School District as a K-12 district. A new school was
built nearby at Jeddito for grades K-12 and another
school at Pinon, to the north of the Hopi Reservation,
for grades K-8. High school students from Pinon are
now bused to Chinle High School, a situation that
will continue until there are enough students to
warrant the building of a high school at Pinon.

The Chinle District had the largest geographical
area of any non-county school district in the southwest. It included the whole northern part of Apache
County beginning north of Ganado, Arizona, and
reaching to the Utah state line. The distance of 80
miles between Chinle High School and Red Mesa High
School created administrative and communication difficulties. The district held an election to form the Red
Mesa Unified School District No. 27 from the northern
part of the original district.

The Long Range Act required the BIA to move
students gradually into the public school system. A
practical solution would have been for the BIA to
operate dormitories and to turn the vacant classrooms over to the public schools, saving the Government millions of dollars in construction money
while providing excellent facilities. As it was, there
were limited funds available to the public schools as

the numbers of students increased. The Bureau continued to receive funds for their construction budget as their student population decreased.

During the 1970's the Bureau changed the system of distributing Johnson-O'Malley funds to a supplementary program, channeling the funding through tribal organizations, which greatly reduced the amount of funds available to the public schools on the reservation. The original legislation was to provide funds for non-taxable lands of the reservations to the public schools.

The BIA did not follow through on turning BIA schools over to public school districts because the Navajo Tribe refused to support the plan. They want to control the finances and to exercise their authority over BIA and public schools. This desire has produced at least one unfortunate consequence. In 1972, the Bureau of Indian Affairs and the Public School District of Tuba City, Arizona, cooperated to develop an amalgamated school system. The BIA had funds for a new boarding high school, and the public school had money for a new high school. To provide a better opportunity for their students, the two schools planned to operate together. The public high school was built adjacent to the BIA high school so that facilities could be shared. There were some facilities that the BIA could build that the public school could not and visa versa. This provided the best of both worlds, each contributing something the other could not.

The administration of the school created some problems during the first few years but it developed into the only Class AAA high school on the reservation. BIA teachers and public school teachers worked with co-principals. Both the local students and the students in the dormitories were taught by BIA and public school teachers.

There was to be a gradual transfer of classroom instruction to the public school while the dormitories and after-school programs were to be managed by the BIA. The transition was never accomplished and in the mid-1980s the tribe assumed the BIA's role in the school. The public school district continued to oper-ate Tuba City High School as an accredited state high school, as the Navajo Tribe contracted with the BIA to cooperatively operate a boarding high school. The Navajo Tribal Education representatives petitioned the local public school board to operate both schools. The Attorney General of Arizona ruled in 1989 that the local legally elected governing board of a public school district could not delegate any of its legal responsibility for a public school to the Navajo Tribe. After much confrontation and a student walk-out during the 1987-88 school year, the cooperative high school became two separate schools. Unfortunately, it is the students who always pay the price for govern-mental power struggles.

Navajo people in a local public school district have a great deal of control over the public schools and the educational programs on the reservation. They vote for school board members who have the authority to bring in Indian administrators, teachers and employees, develop cultural curriculum, and provide parental input. These governing boards can allocate funds, negotiate contracts and determine the organization of the schools. Local Navajos serve on Governing Boards for public schools, as County Board of Supervisors, as State legislators, and are involved as individuals, not as a Tribal Government.[96]

Although the BIA dubbed the public schools the "White man's School" in the early years, it is evident that this can no longer be claimed, since a majority of elected school board members are Navajo. Even so, BIA and Tribal school officials continue to complain that the Navajos have no input in the public schools.

Indian people of other tribes who live and work on the Navajo reservation may be elected to school boards as well as some non-Indian businessmen or their spouses. The governing boards of public schools are the only truly local democratic political entity on the reservation in which all local residents may participate.

Congress has clearly supported the idea of transferring the power of the existing bureaucracy of the BIA to the Indian Tribal bureaucracy through legislation. In 1975, The Indian Self-Determination and Educational Assistance Act (P.L. 93-638) directed the BIA to encourage contract schools with tribal governments. By 1987, 27.8 percent of the total BIA enrollment was in contract schools. The Title XI of the Education Amendments Act of 1978 directed the BIA to facilitate Indian control of Indian Affairs in all matters relating to education; established a contract funding system based upon an equalization formula called the ISEP formula, guaranteeing an amount for each student; directed the BIA to develop a uniform education standard to be established for all BIA and contract schools; changed the employment of teachers and other personnel from the Nationwide Civil Service System to a direct contract basis with each school; reorganized the administration of Education by removing the 12 Agency School Heads from the authority of the Agency Superintendent to the Office on Indian Education Programs in the BIA headquarters, Washington D. C.[97]

Many Navajos and tribal officials feel that schools should not be a local political entity. This is why the Navajo Tribe established a Navajo Nation Education Policy in 1984 which requires the Navajo Division of Education to carry out the laws adopted by the Navajo Tribal Council.[98] It also requires Navajo preference in employment of school and educational personnel in all schools within the Navajo Nation.

The Navajo Tribe adopted the following policy statement: "Navajo Education Standards shall avoid actual conflict with the requirements of state, federal or private accrediting criteria with jurisdiction over the schools *unless* those requirements conflict with an identical educational government requirement of the

Navajo Nation, or unless such conflict is permitted by the external law."[99]

Tacheenie Scott, Biology Professor at Northern Arizona University stated that,

> "There's a VCR rental at every little community on the reservation. The young want a piece of the action, and those of us in education say that if you want it, the key is education.[100]

H. MacArthur Norton, who was acting president for Navajo Community College made these comments:

> "In the 1940', 50's and 60's our culture degenerated.... Fifty percent of our students don't talk Navajo.... We want education... Some see education as an intrusion of ideas. But if we want to remain a sovereign Nation, we will have to take control of education."[101]

When Ross Swimmer was head of the Bureau of Indian Affairs under President Reagan, he recommended that any bureau school not contracted to a tribe become a public school. There were 111 B.I.A. schools and 70 Tribal Contract Schools. The Tribes strenuously objected to this proposal.

Secretary of Education Lauro F. Cavazos and Secretary of the Interior Manual Lujan Jr., appointed by President Bush, made an unprecedented joint visit to five bureau schools in three states. Secretary Lujan stated:

> "It's very clear that the problems you find amongst Indian-education programs are not dissimilar to what you find in the regular

> public-school setting: dropouts,
> low achievement, lack of parental
> involvement."[102]

Secretary Lujan also indicated that he did not think the bureau needed to be restructured and had no plans to phase out schools. His opinion was that the schools had to be operated based on the wish of the local community. Obviously, government and tribal officials continue to perceive locally elected Navajo school board members and public schools as something foreign, not locally controlled.

Unfortunately, they do not seem to be aware of the following facts. The full BIA cost per pupil was $7,917 in 1986. The National was $3,752, Arizona's cost was $3,093 and New Mexico's was $3,195. As funds become more difficult to attain, this BIA figure will become increasingly difficult to justify. Navajo students are gradually moving to the public school system as more roads and schools are constructed. In 1987 there were 16,407 students in BIA funded schools and 22,332 students in public schools on and near the reservation.[103]

In 1988, in a report on Indian Education Programs, the BIA proposed five alternatives: 1). Replace BIA administration of education with a Tribal system of education., 2). Transfer BIA schools to public school districts., 3). Individually contract BIA schools., 4). Issue individual education vouchers., and 5). Revitalize the BIA education system. Whatever they do, as long as the federal government pays the bills, it is inevitable that there will be oversights and demands for accountability will continue. If the state and tribal governments are encouraged by the BIA, it is possible that the BIA will become a grant funding organization, an organization that is primarily concerned with the ways in which others spend its money.[104]

The U.S. Senate's Special Committee on Investigation of the Select Committee on Indian Affairs in 1990 recommended that the Bureau of Indian Affairs be gradually eliminated. The tribes have not received this well, preferring to negotiate with the BIA rather than other branches of government.

An ongoing problem in education is that of re-cruiting and maintaining good professional teachers for the reservation schools. The BIA and the Navajo Tribe have an Indian Preference Rule which requires them to hire a qualified Indian applicant, whether for an initial appointment or an advancement, over a similarly qualified non-Indian applicant. A local tribal advisory board may, on an individual basis, consider a non-Indian if they believe it to be in their best interests.

The Indian Preference rule has not produced any more Indian teachers than other programs. As of 1988 there were 507 full time and 21 part-time BIA teachers on the Navajo Reservation and 39% were Indian.

Congress drastically changed the status of gov-ernment employees when they enacted Title XI of the Education Amendments Act of 1978. Previously, BIA teachers were under the protection of Civil Service regulations. Employment of teachers and other personnel was removed from the Nationwide Civil Service System to a direct contract basis with each school. This effectively eliminated all reemployment rights from these positions.

This contract system has lowered the BIA teacher salaries that once were higher than public school teacher's salaries. In Arizona, the average BIA salary is $19,867 compared to $26,280 for public school teachers. In New Mexico, the average BIA salary is $19,957 compared to $23,977 for public school teach-ers.[105]

Traditionally when non-Indian teachers were sent to the reservation they were expected to serve and then return home, as in any foreign service post. It has always been assumed that, as the Navajo people attained the level of education common to the rest of the nation, all of their teachers would be Navajo. This goal has not been reached, even with an increase in the number of Navajo teachers. Navajo parents surveyed in 1971 indicated that they did not put as much of a premium on having a Navajo teacher as they did on having a teacher who understood and appreciated their children.[106]

The turnover in teacher personnel on the reservation is a true tragedy. The non-Navajo teacher cannot own a home or become a permanent member of the community. Many empathetic, culturally aware and Navajo speaking teachers have left the reservation to buy homes and enjoy the advantage of living in cities off the reservation. Those who retire from the public and government schools leave the area and deprive the community of their wisdom and support. Many professional Navajo teachers prefer to live in cities where they and their children can benefit from the ownership of a home and to take part in the activities available only in cities.

Another continuing problem concerns maintaining the funding level of special federal programs for Indian education. Historically, spending cuts and national emergencies have always eroded funds earmarked for Indian programs. The move to reduce the budget deficit could have a major impact on future planning.

The value of bilingual education is another issue that has yet to be resolved. The national trend to bilingual education has not been fully accepted as a viable way to increase educational achievement for the Navajo student. While there have been some developments at Rough Rock Demonstration School, the primary purpose of the program was cultural awareness and maintenance. Rock Point School, originally a Bureau of Indian Affairs School, and now a contract school run with federal funds, has developed a most comprehensive bilingual program. But the results of the program have not been widely accepted among the other schools on the reservation. Tuba City Public Schools developed and piloted an elementary school bilingual program in the 1960's but the program now seems to be extinct. The problem of finding teachers who are truly bilingual will continue to slow progress in this area. Many Navajo students may never reach their true potential.

All of the educational programs, on and off the reservation, have to address the fact that Navajo students are from one to three years behind the rest of the children in the state and nation on achievement tests. Many explanations for this problem have been advanced. There are those who point out that the tests are culturally biased and should not be used to measure the educational achievement of the Navajo student. This has validity, but if Navajo students do not read and write well in English, many opportunities will never be available to them as they will be in competition with those who have acquired these skills.

The schools on the reservation have enrollments of 85 to 100 percent Navajo students. Thousands of these students start school speaking little or no English. Many do not have electricity, running water, television or libraries in their homes, and only Navajo is spoken. In many other countries, boys and girls learn the skills of reading, writing and computation in their native language while they are learning the official national language. Unfortunately, most Navajo people are not literate in their own language.

Statistics concerning completion of high school and college show that Navajo students are not on a par with national student figures. The latest high school graduation figures show the following data: Nationally, 71.1 percent of high school students graduate, in Arizona, 64.4 percent graduate, and 67 percent of the Navajo students graduate.[107] The dropout rate is 60 percent at the end of the first year in college with 4,323 Navajo students continuing to attend colleges.[108]

Education will continue to offer a mighty challenge
as the decision makers address the reality of the
problems related to it that will require bold but
effective solutions.

CHAPTER ELEVEN

RESERVATION LIVELIHOOD

Navajos include domesticated animals in their religious beliefs because of their importance. Their religious stories tell how animals came to be created for the people, and their value in Navajo life. Livestock has always been valuable and wealth is still measured by the number of animals owned by any person, family or clan. Herds were and still are increased even in times of great hardship. Older people believe that if you ever eat all of your sheep, even during famine, there will be no more sheep.

Livestock was acquired during the 17th century. Traditionally, the mother owned the sheep which she tended and guarded while the men were hunting and raiding. She did the shearing, processing and weaving of the wool. She determined which relatives would help with the flocks. It was the mother who provided the dowry of animals for her daughter so that she would be well established when her new husband came to live with her. She usually sent some animals with her son to his new bride and home.

The horses were owned by the man of the house. He used them for hunting, raiding, and moving belongings. He also provided them to sheep herders and to the mother of the house. Horses were bartered at the Taos yearly fair. Spain gave one horse for twelve to fifteen hides and two pack horses for a slave girl who was ten years old. Horse breeders did well selling and trading their animals.[109]

The Navajos and other neighboring tribes constantly raided the Spanish settlements and each other for horses. This was the most convenient way to obtain them. The favorite time for raiding the horse enclosures was just before sunup, when everyone was still asleep. It gave the raiders all day to distance themselves from any pursuit. By 1775, the horses in New Mexico were so depleted that Spain had to send 1,500 horses to the province. They were to be used for protection against raiding Apaches, Navajos, Comanches, and Utes.[110]

By 1846 it was estimated that the Navajos had over 30,000 head of horned cattle, 500,000 sheep and 10,000 horses and mules. Colonel Kit Carson waged warfare by taking or destroying their animals which had a traumatic effect on the Navajos, causing them to surrender by the hundreds. When the Navajos were released from Fort Sumner in 1868 the government gave them 30,000 sheep and 4,000 goats. These animals were soon mixed in with additional stock shared by relatives who had escaped capture and in 12 short years, by 1880, an Agent estimated that the Navajos had approximately 60,000 horses, 500 mules, 1,000 burros, 500 horned cattle, 1,100,000 sheep and 400,000 goats. These figures were not based on factual surveys. The Navajos no longer raided the settlements or other tribes and they didn't have the resources to buy that many animals.

In 1875 Leicester or Cotswold sheep were introduced by the government to improve the Navajo strain of sheep. In 1880, the Navajos marketed 1,100,000 pounds of wool while retaining an additional 100,000 pounds for their own use in weaving. Wool became a credit bartering system between the early trading posts and the Navajos. There was a growing demand on the reservation for goods from the outside world and the livestock industry became increasingly valuable to the Navajos. The ever increasing numbers of livestock caused the reservation land to become overgrazed and eroded. During the 1880's the reservation was enlarged several times to obtain more grazing land.

Angora rams were purchased in 1899 to improve the quality of goat wool. The estimation of Navajo stock in 1914 included: 1,781,900 sheep, 43,000 cattle, 87,000 horses, 3,795 mules, and 5,440 burros. Livestock continued to increase and when the first grazing survey was taken in 1935 it was evident that the existing reservation lands could only support a maximum of 500,000 sheep. The range was more than 100 percent overstocked and depressed wool and lamb markets were causing the surplus of stock to increase rapidly.

The Navajo economy was very delicate, in view of the fact that it was almost entirely based on the raising of livestock and agriculture. The people were poor and uneducated so they were totally unprepared to understand the nature of grazing problems or the recommended solutions. The proposal to reduce livestock was incomprehensible to the people who had raised livestock for hundreds of years.

The government knew the need for soil conservation and stock water development on the reservation and was willing to spend millions of dollars to carry out the necessary programs. But these programs would be wasted unless the carrying capacity of the grazing lands could be balanced with the correct number of livestock to stop the range deterioration. It became necessary to offer an alternative to the Navajo who would be affected by the reduction of his herd.

The traditional ownership of livestock had never been an equal one. There were those who had vast herds, those with modest herds and those who owned few or no livestock and worked for the large owners. The herders and workers represented a large percentage of the total population and would be affected the most by any reduction.

Commissioner Collier, in 1933, established a five point reduction program: 1) The Navajo Tribal Council was to adopt a resolution sanctioning the reduction of livestock, 2) an attempt would be made to secure additional grazing lands, 3) a soil conservation program would be developed over a large area, 4) an emergency conservation program, already underway, would be continued and 5) an education program containing a provision for the construction of fifty day schools would be launched. The Navajos were told that wages would replace the financial losses by individual stockmen and that improved breeding practices would increase the income from their remaining stock.[111]

The Relief Administration agreed to purchase 100,000 sheep at $1.00 to $1.50 a head for ewes and $2.25 to $3.00 a head for older lambs. The following quotas were established for specific areas of the reservation: 1) 20,000 head for The Northern Agency, 2) 30,000 thousand head for The Southern Agency, 3) 15,000 head for The Eastern Agency, 5) 10,000 head for The Hopi. 6) 8,000 head for The Leupp Agency.

Large stockholders refused to reduce sizable numbers from their herds and insisted that the reduction be carried out with an equal percentage from all herds. The government agreed that every stockholder was to sell 10 percent of his herd with ewes representing 75 percent of that total. This system caused the small stockman to lose good stock and the large stockman to make a good profit on culls. Large stockmen maintained their herds at a peak of productivity while the small stockmen's herds decreased in productivity.[112]

Livestock was the traditional symbol of wealth, rather than money, and the power derived from owning livestock could never equate to the money received for the sale of livestock. During the winter of 1933-34, 90,000 head of sheep or 90 percent of the quota were sold.

The Tribal Council members refused to adopt a goat reduction program without talking to stockmen in 1934. In April, they finally agreed to a reduction

program of 150,000 head of goats. Fifty percent of
all female goats were to be sold at $1.00 a head.
This program started out well enough but the weather
and range conditions delayed the delivery of the
goats at the agreed upon time. The Navajos were
given permission to slaughter and eat as many goats
as they could use. Then the government committed
one of the most uninformed, illogical acts possible;
they slaughtered 3,500 head of goats in Navajo
Canyon and left them to rot.[113]

This senseless slaughter shocked and enraged the
Navajos. They have a traditional respect for the
right of existence of all life forms and an aversion to
wasteful abuse of livestock. To the Navajos, even
though they had sold the animals, this was a senseless destruction of a symbol of their livelihood.
Consequently, only 13,314 goats and 13,866 sheep were
sold in 1935, effectively stopping the reduction
program.[114]

The small stockmen were finally exempted from the
reduction program and range management districts
were established for each 1,000,000 acres of grazing
land. A maximum limit of livestock was established
in each district based on the condition of the land to
be grazed. The Navajo Tribal Council was given
authority to adopt grazing regulations.

The opposition to livestock reduction reached its
highest peak in the 1940's. The first grazing permits
that were issued were based upon the 1937 livestock
ownership count, effectively reducing the grazing
capacity to 500,000 head of sheep. In 1941 the Tribal
Council petitioned for issuance of special grazing
permits to allow the Navajos to retain larger numbers
of livestock. In 1942 the special permits were extended until such time as the Commissioner might act
to rescind them. The regular permit holders who
were not eligible for the special permits were told to
sell all excess livestock by December of 1942. Those
who did not comply would be charged with trespass.
This decision was disputed by those affected, but the

United States District Court in Prescott, Arizona,
handed down an order for the defendants to remove
excess livestock from the reservation range on or
before September 15, 1942.[115]

During the war years, new sources of income
became available to the Navajos. They worked for the
railroads and other industries, changing the Navajo
society and economic structure. The agricultural base
ceased to be a principle source of income for the
majority of the population. Despite the declining
economical importance of raising livestock, its cultural
value to the Navajo people remains to this day . It
is still a most desirable and acceptable way to earn a
living.

The Navajos fought to decrease the grazing regulations following the war period. A temporary freeze
was issued in June of 1948, concerning the punitive
provisions of the Special Grazing Regulations concerning trespass. Ten years of drought and continued overgrazing accelerated the damage to the
grazing lands leaving many acres bare of forage.

In 1948, the Secretary of the Interior stopped
issuing the special grazing permits and withdrew the
punitive measures contained in the Special Grazing
Regulations. The requirements for dipping and
branding livestock were continued. He ordered the
Navajo Tribal Council to complete a revision of the
grazing regulations by July 1, 1948. This deadline,
as with previous deadlines, was not met. In April of
1952, the Navajo Tribal Council requested that the
Secretary: 1) reestablish the special grazing permits,
2) authorize the establishment of Tribal Grazing
Committees in each district, 3) suspend all punitive
provision except for those pertaining to the dipping
and branding of livestock , and 4) withhold amendment of the grazing regulations until all of the Navajo
people could be informed concerning the recommended
changes proposed by the government.[116]

This request was granted in October of 1952. On March 29, 1954, the Advisory Committee adopted a resolution recommending that a draft of proposed revisions to the Grazing Regulations be sent to the Navajo Tribal Council. The Council approved them with minor changes on June 9, 1954. After joint approval by the Bureau and the Tribe, it was then sent to the Secretary of Interior. The Solicitor for the department recommended additional changes which were finally agreed to by the Council on January 27, 1956. The Secretary accepted them on May 1, 1956.

A year later, the Council adopted a resolution requesting an extension of the deadline for reducing the number of livestock for another year. This request was approved by the Secretary. In March of 1958 the Council asked for another extension which was once again approved, moving the date to April 25, 1959.

By November of 1958 the reservation was in critical condition due to the drought and 20,000,000 pounds of grain and feed were distributed to starving livestock. This was the third year of an emergency feeding program. In June of 1959, the grazing conditions on the reservation were severe with virtually no forage on 2,000,000 acres, scarce on 9,300,000 acres. Only 3,150,000 acres of adequate forage was available, with 500,000 acres of abundant forage. Because half of the stock was in terrible condition, the Department of Agriculture conducted an additional emergency feeding program in October of 1960.

A study and analysis of the grazing lands in the summer of 1960 revealed that: 1) 676,000 acres of grazing lands were completely depleted, 2) 5,500,000 acres were severely overgrazed and in danger of becoming depleted, 3) the reservation livestock capacity had now been placed at 387,00 head, 4) the 1959 count of livestock showed 539,323 head of sheep on the grazing lands, 5) the number of grazing permits had increased from 7,954 to 80,557, and 6) that the depleted range suffered an estimated

$5,000,000 in property loss. The government had spent $8,400,000 on emergency feeding programs with no end in sight. That amount of money exceeded the sale value of all of the livestock on the whole reservation. [117]

Even these grave conditions did not force the Tribe to take serious action to limit the number of livestock on the overgrazed reservation ranges. In 1960, 50 percent of the Navajo families had livestock grazing permits although livestock represented only 10 percent of their total income.

Finally, in November of 1960, the Tribal Council authorized $597,000 in an attempt to purchase livestock. Approximately 50,000 sheep were sold and removed from the reservation at a cost of $355,145. For the first time, the Navajos themselves became involved in trying to solve this problem. [118]

Overgrazing and the lack of available food continued to exist for another 30 years, while emergency food for livestock was supplied by the U.S. Department of Agriculture. The Navajo Tribe's efforts to enroll in the emergency feed program for livestock from the U.S. Department of Agriculture was blocked by the Navajo Area BIA in 1990. The BIA agreed to change its position only if the tribe would agree to a viable stock reduction plan. The BIA provided statistics showing that the Navajos are trying to raise 350 percent more livestock than the land is capable of sustaining.

There is a lingering drought, but James Stephens, BIA Area Director for the Navajo Reservation takes the position that the current range conditions were caused by decades of overgrazing, not the drought. If agreement can be reached on his request, 52,000,000 pounds of livestock feed can be obtained, almost free, for the livestock on the reservation. Stephens contends that: "Something has to be done if we are to preserve the land for future generations." [119]

Subsistence stock raising remains an important cultural way of life. Commercial stock raising could be possible someday if several stockholders combined herds and used tribal grazing lands, paying a use fee for the lands. It is doubtful that this will happen but it would provide a good program for range management in which undergrazed areas could be utilized instead of the overgrazed areas.

Relatively few Navajos will be able to continue this way of life. The reservation lands cannot be extended at will by Congress. The loss of considerable acreage to the Hopi Tribe from the joint-use area will further decrease land grazing capacity. The route of education, the acquisition of skills, and cultural adaptations will be forced upon future generations of Navajos. Those who lack education, training and skills will have to subsist on a combination of reservation resources such as farming, livestock raising and welfare. Those with skills and education will not always be able to find employment on the reservation and will be forced to exist on welfare or seek job opportunities off-reservation. For a few, livestock raising will provide a good way of life, with adequate income, in the areas of the reservation with good forage.

The love of livestock is still exhibited by many wage-earning Navajos. They buy livestock with their earnings, planning to become stockmen when they retire from their present jobs.

The largest employers on the reservation are a variety of governmental agencies including the Navajo Tribe, Public School Districts, State Agencies with offices on the reservation and the Bureau of Indian Affairs. Navajo people are employed by such small enterprises as Peabody Coal and other utility related operations on the reservation.The overall unemployment rate is four times that of the rest of the country. In most areas of the reservation, the rate is between 30 and 40 percent.

Chairman MacDonald held two economic conferences that created national attention. The first was the Navajo Economic Summit in August, 1987, to explore the possibility of locating industries on the reservation. It was reported that:

> "MacDonald invited several U.S. Senators, General Dynamics Corporation President Oliver Boiliau, Utah Governor Corey Caruthers and about 15 other government and corporate leaders to the tiny reservation town of Tohatchi, N.M., for the summit."[120]

Chairman MacDonald also held a high-technology conference in October:

> "With a lot of help from friends, MacDonald is playing host to a high-technology conference this weekend at Leupp, a reservation town 50 miles east of Flagstaff.
>
> Representatives of government and industry from throughout the United States will be in attendance in that unlikely locale, attracted by the dynamic Navajo leader and his co-hosts, Hewlett-Packard Chairman Daniel Packard and former Senator Barry Goldwater.
>
> MacDonald wants to lead the Navajo Nation into the future by attracting high-technology business to the reservation. His banner reads: 'Navajo Means Business'."[121]

It is doubtful that industry will be enticed to locate on the reservation for several reasons. Most successful industries are operated by highly skilled professionals. There are large numbers of unemployed workers in the major cities of the southwest.

Many industries are moving to the Sunbelts of the
nation in order to attract the top professionals that
they need for their operations. These locations offer
a lifestyle that highly trained and skilled professionals desire. It is unlikely that industries located on
or near the reservation could offer the same sort of
lifestyle hundreds of miles from major cities. Employees living on the reservation could not own a
home and the advantages of the cultural and social
activities of a large city would not be readily available.

Most Navajos do not have and probably will not
have the level of skilled professional training to
operate these industries. If or when they acquire
such training, they probably will want the same
advantages that a non-Navajo wants.

Two large business employers rate their Navajo
workers very highly in attendance and competence.
Peabody Coal Company gives their Navajo employees
high marks and states that they have the lowest
absence rate of any coal company in the country.
Peabody employees 900 people, 90 percent of whom
are Navajo. Their pay is from $30,000 to $40,000 a
year. The per-capita income on the Navajo Reservation
in 1988 was $2,424 which is about 72 percent below
the national average.[122]

Bashas, a Phoenix-based supermarket chain, has
five stores on the Navajo Reservation. Bashas reports
that nearly all of their employees, including managers,
are Indian and that they perform their jobs extremely
well. Bashas stores are located on the reservation
because they wanted to be there. The Navajo people
needed services and jobs and Bashas wanted to be
part of the solution addressing those needs.

Tourism is one local industry that has begun to
develop employment opportunities for Navajos. There
has been a tremendous growth in visitors to all of
the Navajo parks and surrounding areas. The individual bead and jewelry entrepreneurs along the

highways are very busy during the summer, with cars and motor homes parked around their stands and tourists buying their products.

A new industry on Indian reservations is snow-balling across the United States, making millions of dollars for tribes while allowing them   complete freedom to spend it as they wish.   Indians, due to their trust and treaty status, have been given the capacity to develop gambling on their reservations by the federal government. The nearest casino to the Navajos is located at Towaoc, on the Ute Mountain Reservation southwest of Cortez, Colorado.

The state of Arizona has laws forbidding gambling casinos, but those laws will be changed soon.   The Governor's representative is busy negotiating agreements for casinos with tribes other than the Navajo. The big players in this enterprise are the successful Eastern Indian tribes and the professional gamblers from Nevada who are being employed by tribes as advisors, and possibly as the   builders and operators of casinos, on their reservations.   Tom Laughlin, who founded Laughlin, Nevada, across the Colorado River from Bull Head City, Arizona, has just signed a contract with the Mohave Indians, south of Bull Head City, to develop and operate a tribal casino.

The Navajo Tribal Council has not initiated the necessary actions to enter this business, but the Navajos at Page, Arizona, and other areas are already pressuring it to begin building casinos. They believe that the casinos will create employment and provide funds for their tribes. The Fort McDowell Apache Reservation near Phoenix has a bingo hall and a casino, and the Apache tribe paid each of its members $4,000 from its first gambling profit.

One can imagine the glamour that would be associated with a large resort hotel with casino accommodations standing high on the red sandstone bluffs overlooking Lake Powell, in northern Arizona.   There would be a golf course, horse stables, hiking trails,

bus tours, lake cruises, fishing and swimming. Attractive Navajo men and women dressed in traditional
clothing would conduct tours and hold seminars
concerning Navajo culture. There would be an open
market where local Navajos could sell their wares to
the tourists.

Navajo men and women, also dressed in traditional
Navajo costume, could work as dealers in the Casinos.
There might be groups of dancers and singers performing in different parts of the resort. A special 90
minute performance of Indian Dancers could be one of
the main show highlights in a large theater that
would duplicate the appearance of a hogan. The
customers could dine on fried bread and beans or
Navajo tacos before the entertainment. This would
provide a great family vacation spot where mom and
dad could also gamble in the convenient casino.

Since there is presently a law prohibiting the sale
of liquor on the Navajo reservation, the Navajo Tribal
Council would have to amend its laws to allow alcoholic beverages to be sold in the resort. And, although
the establishment of casinos may be a boon to members of the tribe, the gambling industry is a two-
edged sword. This activity will generate so much
money that it will require carefully controlled and
monitored operations to protect the tribe's interests
in the new industry.

CHAPTER TWELVE

HEALTH PROBLEMS

Smallpox was a constant threat to the health of all Indians due to their lack of natural immunity. The Navajos were not exempt from its influence. Though there were epidemics during the Spanish periods, the life style of the Navajos probably protected them from the ravages of the disease that the Puebloans suffered. There is some evidence of dental and bone diseases, birth defects and tuberculosis.

When in captivity at Fort Sumner, the health of the Navajos deteriorated badly. They were without adequate food and shelter and disease was rampant. They made every effort to avoid the hospital because of their dread of the spirits of those who died there.

In 1870, some 2,134 men, 1,753 women and 2,028 children were vaccinated against smallpox. They had been vaccinated in 1855 and many were found to still be immune. Nearly 9,000 Navajos were eventually vaccinated. One epidemic struck in 1899 and another in 1901. Each caused deaths but were not as disastrous as they would have been without the previous vaccinations.

The first missions on the Navajo reservation and adjacent areas were hospitals and clinics. There is little data concerning the extent of early health services provided by the government after the return from Fort Sumner. In the 1930's, health services were found to be inadequate and they were increased by the government, but the funding never seemed to be adequate for the needs. Small hospitals were eventually established at Shiprock, Fort Defiance, Tuba City, Winslow and Chinle.

In the 1950s, the children and people in the outlying communities were visited regularly by nurses who traveled to various day schools, as did dentists. Very few services were provided in these outlying areas. Nevertheless, the days when the nurse and dentist came were big community events. The little community schools were usually run by a husband and wife teaching team with the help of dormitory attendants, a cook and a janitor. Traders and their families often completed the community. Many of the Navajos used this day to come to the store to trade as well as to visit the school to see the medical person or just to watch the proceedings and visit.

At the school, the nurse and her driver/interpreter examined people who were ill or injured and determined if they needed first aid or needed to see a doctor. If it was a serious situation, the nurse transported the person back to the hospital. She immunized the students, treated them for skin diseases and restocked the medicine cabinets with bandages, medications, and other materials needed by the teachers to treat minor health problems.

The teachers and aids held sick call each morning before classes began. Most teachers utilized this period as a time to reinforce health and cleanliness practices. Students were taught to brush their teeth, comb their hair, and to care for their fingernails. Those who had impetigo, ring worm, head lice, and infected sores were treated. During periods of high hepatitis concern students were examined to see if they had "blue eyes", a ploy to check the whites of the eyes for signs of jaundice, which often accompanies hepatitis. Children with temperatures and serious ailments were then transported to the nearest hospital, usually on an out patient basis. This meant requiring a staff member--a teacher, an aide or the janitor, to drive the students a distance of 50 to 80 miles, depending upon the location of the school.

The dentist and his assistant/interpreter visited the school once a year and twice if it was possible.

They brought a portable dental chair and large wooden cases filled with their dental tools and supplies. The children's teeth were checked in the morning and then treated as necessary.

This was usually the first visit to a dentist for many children, and extensive treatment was often needed. In these cases, the dentist would schedule a visit to the nearest hospital for the work. It was not unusual for a student to have several cavities filled in addition to having extractions. Some students had multiple extractions. For many, it was not a happy day on campus.

Time permitting, the dentist would see the staff and others from the community who had dental problem. He treated some and referred others to the dental clinic at the nearest hospital.

Some schools lacked the luxury of electricity so the dentist was equipped with a treadle-powered drilling machine. By the end of the day the dentist and his assistant were usually exhausted from operating the treadle. Medication was left for those who had serious work performed on their teeth.

By the time the Long-Range Rehabilitation Act was enacted in 1950, the Navajos were particularly afflicted with tuberculosis, pneumonia and diarrheal diseases. Facilities to care for these problems were few and far between. The Long-Range Rehabilitation Act provided for the following actions. The BIA was directed: 1) to remodel and expand facilities at Shiprock, Tuba City, Winslow and Chinle to attain 104 beds for general purposes and 250 for tuberculosis, 2) to establish a system of field stations or clinics in conjunction with the larger reservation boarding schools, 3) to develop itinerant medical and dental services and 4) to provide an adequate health program with emphasis on curative services in general and on tuberculosis in particular.

By 1954, a new 75 bed hospital had been complet-

ed at Tuba City and contracts had been signed with
ten state and private sanitaria for 500 tuberculosis
patients in Arizona, California, and New Mexico.[123]

While the Bureau of Indian Affairs was making
further plans, Congress passed Public Law 568 which
transferred full responsibility for Indian Health
Programs to the Public Health Service in the Department of Health, Education and Welfare as of July 1,
1955.

One health problem that plagued boarding school
students was hepatitis. It was a constant concern to
all who worked with these children. In the late 1950s,
Tuba City Boarding School had to be closed because
more than 80 percent of the students had hepatitis.
The well students were sent home and the dormitories
became hospital wards, with teachers helping to care
for students who would have been in their classrooms.

The Division of Indian Health set a goal to elevate
the health status of the Navajos to a point which
compared favorably with that of the nation as a
whole. It established a program of intensified, integrated service that covered preventive as well as
rehabilitative care, with attention to the whole disease
spectrum and to the whole cycle of life from prenatal
care to geriatric services. This program required
additional facilities, additional personnel and the creation of more services with new categories of health
workers to operate them.

A new 75 bed hospital was constructed at Shiprock. A 200 bed base hospital was built at Gallup,
New Mexico, to be the referral center for reservation
facilities. Tuberculosis care was provided in a facility in Albuquerque, New Mexico, and in several
community and state hospitals on a contractual basis.
A small facility was retained in Fort Defiance, Arizona.

Health Centers were constructed at outlying areas
of Chinle, Kayenta, Tohatchi, Pinon, White Cone, Round

Rock, Cornfields and Pueblo Pintada. An adequate number of employees' living quarters were furnished at those locations.

The Division of Indian Health developed a completely integrated approach to health programs, providing not only personnel usually associated with medicine, but specialists to meet unique needs as well as many auxiliary workers in supportive positions. Doctors and specialists who had worked with many similar illnesses, in foreign countries with national health organizations, came to the reservation. Additional services were contracted through community, state and private hospitals and clinics. Qualified Navajos were trained and assigned to health facilities.

However, the health service programs suffered the same employee problems as the educational services. The majority of the medical staff, particularly medical doctors, psychologists, and skilled technicians were supplied by the United States Health Service. Most medical doctors were serving a two year period in the public health service instead of the military in return for federal assistance during their medical education. When their two year period was up, they returned to the outside world to enter private practice. Therefore, many of them never became a part of the community, and never participated in civic affairs. The career public health personnel were the exception in that many of them stayed for a longer period of time, but they eventually moved to promotional assignments at other public health facilities.

The Health Committee of the Navajo Tribal Government actively participates in programs for their people. There are programs for disease control, environmental sanitation , eye glasses, prosthetic aids and for the encouragement of young Navajos to obtain health training and to return to work with their own people. There are a few Navajo medical doctors working with the health organization and the Navajo people.

Field medical programs have become more available and nearer to the people through field health stations, school health programs and home visitations. There are now enforceable sanitation codes that apply to trading posts, privies and homes. Vaccinations are available for rabies control, fly and insect control is addressed and sanitary home water supply units have been developed. Housing areas are being built in many isolated reservation areas with running water, sewers and electricity. Hospital admissions are growing. Higher average daily patient census and increasing visits to dental offices indicate more acceptance by the Navajos.[124]

Funding the programs now in existence will be a continuing problem for the government as the Navajo population continues to grow and other pressures for funds are brought to bear on Congress for services for the rest of the nation. Some modification may be made if those Navajos who can afford treatment pay for that service. Many are covered by medical insurance but still receive free medical treatment. The only qualification to receive treatment is proof that the patient has one-quarter degree of Indian blood.

Non-Indian people have begun to accept the fact that the traditional beliefs of the Navajo are an important part of their well being. Public Health administrators have encouraged the use of Hatathlies for selected problems to ease patients' minds about coming to a medical facility. The prisons in Arizona have authorized Navajo Hatathlies to visit Navajo prisoners to conduct curing ceremonies.

As the Navajo population attains more education and has closer contact with the outside world, the strength of traditional religious life is threatened. The power of a Hatathlie is based on his ability to conduct a ceremony correctly using special herbal medicines.. Every time an old Hatathlie dies, some ceremonies, techniques and skills disappear. The medicinal practices of the Navajos are not written but are memorized and passed on verbally from generation to generation.   There are fewer young men and women understudying the practitioners.

It is not unusual to see people drinking and being rude at ceremonials.   In 1990, Hatathlies and members of the Native American Church asked the Navajo Tribal Police for more protection at their night ceremonies.   Other church groups were afraid to have night ceremonies for fear that they would attract those who only want to get drunk and disrupt the services.[125]   Many times older people scold the audiences and plead with them for better behavior. They remind the people that the ceremonies are performed for health reasons.

The financial burden of feeding all of the people in attendance has been a factor in the disappearance of some ceremonies.   The Fire Dance is rarely conducted due to the length of the ceremonial and the large crowds that must be fed.   As many as four or five thousand people attend a fire or corral dance for nine days and nights. It is economically impossible for the traditional people, who usually are the ones who believe in the power of the ceremonies, to sponsor them.   They are the people with the least education and the least financial resources.

Because nine day ceremonies are so costly, there are more three and five day ceremonies.   The shorter ceremonies are not inexpensive.   Good friends and relatives bring gifts of food such as flour, lard, mutton, potatoes, onions, and fruit.   These items are delivered to the cooking area where they are greatly appreciated by the family.

It has been many years since the author has heard of a fire or corral dance being held.   The ceremony may cease to exist as the Hatathlies who perform it die.   When there are no families requesting it, the Hatathlies cannot pass on their knowledge of this ritual.

Some ceremonials have been described in written

form to preserve and maintain the information. But the specific details of how to perform all of the songs, prayers, sandpaintings, medications, and ritu- als have not been documented. Many young Hatathlies do not know how to use the traditional herbal medi- cines for curing illnesses.

Many of the younger generation have turned away from the old traditions of religious healing, losing their faith in the old ways. But they have failed to discover a substitute for the loss of their religion. In their new life, they live in a gray world where things are neither black nor white. The loss of self-identity causes many social ills among these people. With more and more Navajos moving from their home sites to reservation sub-divisions, or even off the reserva- tion to seek work, traditional values are being erod- ed. It is difficult to find experienced Hatathlies in urban areas. However, many Navajos believe that even in the face of urbanization, the old ways will survive.[126]

There has been a dramatic improvement in the health of the people in the past thirty-five years. The birth rate on the Navajo reservation is one of the highest in the United States at 2.7 percent. This, combined with an improved infant mortality rate, will provide a fast growing population. The Navajo Nation is becoming a young nation as the youth now outnumber the elderly, a condition which will differ from the nation's population for some time to come. The median age on the reservation in 1990 was 18.7 years.

The Navajo is totally dependent upon federal so- cialized medicine. Even though some wage earners seek dental and medical services in neighboring cities, the mass of the population is dependent upon the generosity of the federal government and the whims of Congress.

Personnel in the U.S. Public Health Service on the Navajo reservation did some excellent research that improved the health of many Navajo people. They became involved with the research for a more satis- factory treatment of tuberculosis. The medication that was developed allowed children with tuberculosis to attend school instead of being isolated in a sanitari- um. Research on the repair of ear drums destroyed by infection made it possible to improve or restore the ability to hear for many people. Their research on mental impairment caused by physical damage to children under the age of three, due to multiple experiences of severe dehydration, was reinforced during similar research by health organizations in third world countries.

A recent study on health problems of the Navajos reflects the influence of modern day society. Navajos, more than most Americans, are likely to be stricken by radiation related diseases, bubonic plague and streptococcal infections.

There are from 150-200 abandoned uranium mines and four deadly uranium dumps at four closed processing mills. The mill residues, if untreated, are still 80 percent as radioactive as when the tailings were buried, creating a cancer-causing "radon" gas which is carried by the wind. The mill tailings at Rare Metals, near Tuba City, and others have been treated with a protective covering. Four families have been moved from the Oak Springs Community where they built their homes using stones from the uranium mill dump.

The majority of all bubonic plague victims in the United States live on the Navajo reservation. It has been reported that 60 percent of the patients who go to Navajo health clinics have strep-related illnesses. Rheumatic fever and rheumatic heart disease, often developing as a result of untreated streptococcal infections, are 25 percent higher in Navajos than in the general population. [127]

A cure for alcoholism continues to be one of the Navajo's most pressing health problems. The sale of

alcoholic beverages is prohibited on the reservation,
so bootleggers get rich from their fellow men. Non-
Navajos have established liquor stores close to the
boundaries of the reservation in all states, causing
cries of protest. Some successful legal actions have
been taken against these stores. Many Navajos have
lost their jewelry and other possessions to satisfy
their need for alcohol. It is difficult to discover a
satisfactory approach to the problems of the Navajos,
when the same problems affect many of the national
population as well. There must be a better system
than the present one. As it now happens, when a
Navajo has liquor on the reservation, the bottle is
opened and the cork is thrown away. The liquor is
quickly consumed so that the person will not be
caught with the bottle and fined or sent to jail.
Programs financed by tribal, state and federal governments have been initiated . In spite of all of
these efforts it still remains an issue in the health
and well-being of the people:

In an article carried by the Arizona Republic, it
was stated that:

> "In Gallup, N.M., a city of 20,000
> that bills itself as the `Indian Capital
> of the United States,' there is one
> alcohol-related death a day, city
> policemen say. There were 2,622 cases
> of people held in jail overnight to dry
> out last year, 80 percent of them were
> Indians.
>
> Surrounding McKinley County's
> alcohol mortality rate is in the top 1
> percent of the nation's 3,100 counties
> according to police figures."[128]

It is unlikely that the problem will be eliminated
until certain social and cultural conditions on the
reservation are remedied. It is obvious that prohibi-
tion has only made money for bootleggers while fail-
ing to reduce alcoholism.

CHAPTER THIRTEEN

CULTURAL CONFLICTS

Positive events are in store for the Navajo Nation. A substantial base of educated and experienced Navajo leadership is developing. Congress continues to act as a supporter and protector of the Navajo Indians. The concept of self-determination is increasingly supported by the nation for all Indians. More and more state funds are being channeled into the reservation areas. It is apparent that the Navajos will benefit from water rights being currently decided by the federal government. The natural resources of oil, gas, coal and manpower will become more and more valuable in future years.

There has been a surge of interest in Navajo culture in the United States. Navajo jewelry has become a standard investment that is much in demand. Navajo artists are producing work that is displayed worldwide. Navajo moccasins, clothing designs, and motifs are wide spread throughout the nation. People want the Navajos to acquire self-determination and to succeed.

However, the Navajo people will still be facing problems that are hard to imagine by anyone not familiar with their present situation. These problems will be an ever present danger to the Navajos and to the rest of the nation unless they are resolved.

Unemployment will continue to be a major concern to the Navajos. Their per-capita cash income is a fraction of the national average and their population is growing at four times the national rate. These factors project a gloomy economic picture that will continue far into the future. There remains a great need for improvement in housing, health conditions and programs for adults.

Non-Indians need to understand that something that is good for one tribe may not be good for another. They also need to know the difference between BIA or government action and that of the Tribal Council. When there are altercations between Indian groups, non-Indians are confused because they only understand "White" against "Red." Tribalism is not understood by most people in the United States so they don't realize that one Indian tribe's worst enemy can be another Indian tribe. Indians served as tried and true army scouts for the white man against other Indians. One of Arizona's first Congressional Medal of Honor recipients was Alchesay, a Chiricahua Apache Indian Scout.

The news media must understand that when the BIA or the Tribal Council takes a stand or an action, it is the established legal authority. Individual urban militant Indians only represent themselves or an urban organization. The media might ask an urban Cherokee what he thinks about a Hopi reservation problem and print his answer as though he knows what is best for the Hopis. Many urban Indians have lost their language, their religion, and their culture. They do not have reservation homes or ties. The needs of those living on the reservation are totally different from the needs of the urban dweller.

Consider the various episodes involving Russell Means, a former leader of the American Indian Movement. He has surfaced in Chinle on the Navajo Reservation, married to a Navajo woman. He employed his usual tactics of railing at the BIA and authority in general when he accused the BIA of putting MacDonald out of office and violating Indian rights. In Window Rock, he tried to make a citizen's arrest of the Agency Superintendent, who is Indian.

Leonard Haskie, the interim chairman of the Navajo Tribe, disagreed with Mean's interpretation of what was happening.

> "MacDonald was removed by the
> majority members of the Navajo Tribal
> Council, not the BIA.", he said.[129]

A general reaction to Means action and Haskie's
answer was summed up in this editorial:

> "This makes no impression on Mr.
> Means. He says that he and pro-
> MacDonald forces plan to hold a
> demonstration in Gallup, New Mexico,
> tomorrow to force the BIA officials to
> apologize to the Navajo people. An
> apology from the BIA is due, but
> for its years of dereliction. None is
> due Mr. MacDonald or his camp fol-
> lowers, and Mr. Means who seems to
> crave attention more than justice for
> the Indians should butt out."[130]

Members of AIM recently protested at Big Mountain in the Navajo-Hopi dispute concerning the removal of Navajo livestock from the Hopi lands. The
leader of the protest was a Navajo who blamed the
BIA for the action. He neglected to take into consid-
eration the fact that the Hopis had won a lawsuit that
ordered the Navajos to remove their livestock. AIM
took sides in an Indian against Indian confrontation.

A controversy developed between some traditional
Navajos and the National Forest Service concerning
the enlargement of recreational facilities on the San
Francisco Peaks near Flagstaff, Arizona. A ski lodge,
lift and parking facility were developed on the west
side of the peaks with a permit from the United
States Forest Service. Developers have recently
requested permission to expand the facilities. This
has happened several times in the past. Each time
various members of the Hopi and Navajo tribes have
protested on the grounds that the mountains are
sacred in their religious beliefs. The claims were
made in reference to a recent law that declared any
public land that is religious ground to any Indian

tribe must be protected under the theory of religious freedom. But one religion cannot be favored over another, including that of the Indians. Permission for the expansion was eventually granted by the courts.

It seems inconsistent that large uranium mining operations are being carried out on Mount Taylor, another sacred mountain, near Grants, New Mexico. These mining operations have been going on for many years without protests from religious leaders. It seems that the disruption of the land on Mount Taylor should create the same religious concerns that recreational developments do on the San Francisco Peaks.

Another area of conflict has been expressed by various Indian people in the news media about the collections of their ancestors' remains by non-Indians in places like the Smithsonian Institute in Washington D.C. However, one must remember that the ruins from which many of the remains were taken were present on Navajo land before it was occupied by Navajos. The methods of dating artifacts bear out the fact that many of the ruins were unoccupied from about 900 to 1100 A.D. and the present Athapascans probably started to move into the area of New Mexico between 1400 and 1500 A.D.

A recent editorial in the Arizona Republic puts this concern in proper perspective. It was written in response to Clara Spotted Elk who did a guest column in the New York Times. She is not Navajo but expresses comments made by many young urban Indian people, including some Navajos in Arizona.

The pertinent parts of her article are quoted here:

> "Ms. Spotted Elk, an American Indian is concerned about the 18,500 Indian remains stored away 'unceremoniously.' she tells us, in the Smithsonian's Natural History Museum in Washington. She sees this as a sacri-

lege.

`Indian people are tired of being specimens,' she says. `Like people the world over, one of our greatest responsibilities is the proper care of the dead.'

Indians, she thinks, are being denied this right. The graves of her ancestors are being desecrated, and American Indians are `outraged' by it.

`We will not accept grave-robbing and the continued hoarding of our ancestor's remains,' she writes.

Some may find me insensitive, but Ms. Spotted Elk's reasoning strikes me as foolish and tendentious.

If the Smithsonian were holding the skeletal remains of identifiable family members--displaying an embalmed Sitting Bull or Crazy Horse perhaps her concern would be legitimate.

But this is far from the case. The Indian remains in the Smithsonian's attic are in no way comparable to the remains of Ms. Spotted Elk's grandfather or mine--people with whom we have close family ties and of whom we may have fond memories.

The bones Ms. Spotted Elk wants liberated are of another order entirely.They are more nearly analogous to the fossil remains of Homo habilis, that remote ancestor of man whose parts have been patiently spooned out of the Olduvai Gorge by the

Leakeys and other paleoanthropolo-
gists.

When Ms. Spotted Elk visited
the Smithsonian several years ago,
as she tells us she did, and was
shown a drawer full of jumbled
Indian bones, she may have conjured
up visions of ancient plains men roaming the wilderness and feeding on
great herds of buffalo.

But if so, this is a credit to her
imagination, not to any family
recollection. The individuals whose
skeletal remains cause her such grief
are unidentifiable and, for the most
part, lived hundreds of years ago.

Such bones are mere objects of
scientific interest, much like the
tanned body of an ancient Briton,
pickled in ooze, that was pulled out
of a peat bog a few years ago.

Englishmen did not storm the
laboratories where this curiosity was
being studied, demanding that their
ancestor be interred in Westminster
Abbey. They regarded the remains as
what they were--an interesting anthropological find.

The Smithsonian does not treat
its Indian collection irreverently.
The remains are not stuffed, decorated with buckskin and feathers and
hung up for gawking tourists to
admire.

The bones Ms. Spotted Elk wants
returned for burial are classified for
future reference and stored in cabinets. They are inaccessible to the

public, but available for students of
aboriginal Americans.

Few will defend the white man's
mistreatment of the Indians, whose
hunting grounds were taken and
whose tribes succumbed first to the
white man's diseases and then to his
superior fire power.

But modern Indians can only
benefit from the study of these
ancient remains.

Instead of urging that the past be
buried, they should want it resur-
rected so that early cultures can
be better understood.

Only then will American Indians
take their rightful place in the history of this continent."[131]

The ruins that we see in the southwest today
were not early Athapascan, pre-Navajo or pre-Apache.
The Navajo Tribal Council has no interest in the
remains from those ruins. The remains of 30 Navajos
are stored at the Smithsonian, mostly collected by the
army during Navajo captivity at Fort Sumner. They
are not identifiable as members of any existing family.
The Navajos have no space to bury their dead and
Navajo families have to search for a place to bury
their loved ones. Most end up burying their relatives on their land, a practice that is illegal without
permission from the tribe. Families, believing that
the burial must take place within three days of death
bury them anyway, feeling that they have no choice.

The Navajo Tribe does not see much logic in
removing the remains from their present storage only
to re-store them on the reservation until a burial
site can be found. It hopes to acquire a section of
the new cemetery at Fort Defiance for this purpose,
but no one can say for sure when that might be.[132]

There are many ruins and archeological sites on the Navajo reservation. Some are large multi-storied cliff dwellings, others are small ruins with storage areas built under rock overhangs with stones. Some may even be found perched atop red sandstone mesas.

Occasionally these ruins have been used by the Navajos as shelter for their livestock and storage of feed. Many times Navajos find pottery near and in the ruins and if it is whole, smash it to let out evil spirits.

Others have used the stones from the ruins to build homes and sheep pens. Although traditional Navajos shun these places because of their fear of the dead, many of the younger people do not feel these restrictions. There is a very lucrative business in selling Anasazi artifacts in the surrounding areas.

There is a difference between the younger and older Indians in their needs and desires . This presents a problem that was best pointed out by Albert Attocknie, Chief of the Comanche Tribe, in a speech he made in Denver, Colorado, in 1944. Although the speech was made almost 50 years ago, the basic problems and differences are still in evidence. The speech earned him a standing ovation and though he is not Navajo, the feelings he expressed have been overheard by the author being repeated by older Navajo people. The fact that the average age for the Navajo reservation now is 18.8 years further emphasizes the problem. Chief Attocknie stated it effectively when he said:

> "I am ignorant, but I have the interest of the young and educated Indians at heart. I came here following the young men from my jurisdiction. I came here especially to see the young and educated Indians organize to help the Indian people.

I hope that when you young educated
Indians take up the question of
organizing for the benefit of Indians,
you will remember that the Indians
are from different classes. There are
Indians like myself who are not educated. Who are restricted and who
cannot exist under conditions that
will work well with the young and
educated Indians.

In the Comanche custom, young
people are referred to as sons and
daughters, so I want to say a few
words along that line. Attempts
have been made to take away the
guardianship of the Indian Bureau
over Indian land. I am opposed to
that; and the reasons given for
lifting the guardianship of the
Indian Bureau from the Indians
especially to aid the uneducated
Indians, is not fair. There is no
reason given why that should be fair.
Now we are very proud of you, our
children, that are so highly educated.
Your oratory here is about as good
as I have ever heard anywhere
including the halls of Congress. You
are able Indians, but the advancement
and achievement obtained by you
educated Indians does not help us
old folk any longer. Our status as
Indians remains the same. You are
highly educated--that does not help
us any at all. My boy's status
does not save my status as an
Indian, as a ward of the Government.

I want you to take this resolution
that was offered here by the Chairman and insert therein words and
language that will help old Indians
like myself. In Oklahoma, the old

Indians are the minority. The young people have such a great majority that we never have any chance to put in the by-laws, rules that we want, because the young and educated people have such a big majority that they rule us out. I would not be here if it was left to the majority. We do not question the legality of majority rule, but it is not fair. The leadership of the council is given to the young, well educated people in my jurisdiction, a lot of them landless.

Those young men really are not interested in an allotted Indian's lands or problems. That is not fair. We don't want to have control of the young, educated Indians, but we want to be represented and be given equal representation in the council affairs and before the Indian Bureau and Congress. We can't do it under the present system, which is legal but not fair. Now I live on a farm. Suppose somebody quits farming, leaves the farm, and goes away somewhere, and then tells me how the farm should be carried on. It is just as fair as that the younger and disinterested Indians rule the Tribes. I think it is very much the same in other tribes in other states. I have been talking for a number of years. Some of you come from closed reservations but you people who have allotted lands will understand what I mean.

It will not be long before the old Indian will be out of sight. I wish to ask young and educated Indians to consider this resolution carefully for the older Indians benefits.

> The Indian Bureau should be
> retained for the protection of the
> aged and allotted landowners. At
> least for awhile, because the old
> man standing before you will, before
> long, pass on to follow my father's
> your father's and your mother's trails
> to that Happy Hunting Ground in
> the realms of the mysterious hereaft-
> er. I thank you."[133]

For many years the tribal councils were dominated
by elder statesmen who were experienced in working
with the government and who were representative of
the large stockmen on the Navajo Reservation. In
recent years the age of councilmen has steadily
decreased. The political actions of representatives in
Indian government are highly visible now and this
causes problems with constituents much like the non-
Indian politician. Some of the expressions of feelings
by Indians have a familiar ring to them.

In the early 1970's a modern group of Indians
burst upon the scene of this nation. They at first
preached the return to the old ways, to relearn the
culture and beliefs. Then they occupied and sacked
the Bureau of Indian Affairs in Washington, D. C. on
November 2, 1972, destroying many irreplaceable
Indian artifacts and records. In 1973, they seized
and occupied Wounded Knee on the Ogalala Sioux
Indian Reservation. In 1975 they initiated an armed
takeover of a Fairchild semiconductor plant in Shiprock, New Mexico.

The organization has been primarily city-oriented,
led by urban Indians who follow the tactics of other
militant-minority civil-rights movements. The leaders
such as Vernon and Clyde Bellacourt, Russell Means,
Dennis Banks and Leonard Peltier are well known.
Peltier, put in prison to serve two life terms for
killing two federal agents in South Dakota, has been
recently released on parole.

AIM leaders have traveled world wide to denounce

perceived wrongs. They appeared before the Russell Tribunal of the United Nations in the Netherlands, met with the Palestine Liberation Organization leader Yasser Arafat in Lebanon and have led protests in most Indian communities and areas.

Presently, AIM seems to have no national leader, but many urban Indians support the organization. AIM is not as popular with Indians living on reservations, especially the duly elected Indians in tribal government and positions of authority. The Navajo Tribal Council refused to allow AIM to hold a conference on the Navajo Reservation after the incident at Shiprock in 1975. The Tribal Chairman came under criticism for the way in which the tribal police were ordered to handle the situation. It remains to be seen if there will be a growth of AIM on the Navajo Reservation, and if so, what purpose it will serve.

People tend to imitate those whom they admire, like or find intriguing. In recent years there has been a growing demand for Indian jewelry, pottery, paintings, sculpture and clothing. Visitors to the reservation have increased dramatically.

For years, sports teams have adopted such names as Braves, Warriors, Redskins, Indians, and Seminoles. It has been reported that some Indians are protesting the use of these names, calling them insulting and derogatory. And yet, these names were originally chosen because they suggest strength, bravery and a fighting spirit. The word "squaw" was borrowed from the Algonquin language and denotes "woman." Yet some object to its use. The list of words goes on and on, but having been taken directly from the language of Indians, how can they be demeaning?

During the 1930's, in a period before Indians became "popular", a group of Boy Scouts in La Junta, Colorado, began to study Indian dances. Each summer they visited different tribes, learned their dances and copied their costumes. The group practiced until all of the steps were correct and accept-

able.   The boys made their own costumes, paying for
the materials and their summer program by putting
on performances at various   functions in public
auditoriums, at fairs, in school gymnasiums, and in
parades.

They traveled and performed in many states for
years.   Eventually, they were criticized by some
urban Indians and accused of making fun of the
Indian religion by copying dances and costumes.
Perhaps it is time for these critics and others to
learn that: "Imitation is the sincerest form of
flattery!"

When newsmen covered the hearings for Chairman
MacDonald, a Navajo was reported to have asked,
"What are all you whites doing out here on our
reservation?"   Bigotry can cause problems with any
group.   The answer supplied by a white physician
on the reservation and which appeared in the Arizona
Republic portrays a true perspective of the reactions
from those trying to help the Navajos progress into
the future.   It was expressed most eloquently:

> "Let me list a few of the things
> that we whites, blacks, Hispanics, and
> yellows are doing. We are the re-
> porters who uncovered   the greed
> and   dishonesty of your   tribal lead-
> ers. We   are the doctors,   dentists,
> nurses, physical   therapists, pharma-
> cists, etc., who try to keep you
> healthy. We   are   the technicians who
> keep your technology running, the
> lights on and the telephones working.
> We are the pilots that   fly   the
> emergency   flights to   save Navajo
> lives. We   are   the tax payers   who
> pay for your   schools, roads, and
> other   services Navajos receive from
> non-Indians who pay taxes you are
> exempt from.   We are the people   who
> believe in honesty   in government.
> Such a racist remark is an embarrass-

> ment to all of the good Navajos we
> work and live with, and to many good
> people of all colors who are here to
> help."[134]

There are still those tribal members who are militantly anti-white. They should realize that there are more whites who are positive than negative in their attitudes toward the Navajos. It doesn't make good sense to alienate those supportive people with racist remarks. Navajo people, with their complex legal status and unique geographical location, are tied to the United States, Utah, New Mexico and Arizona as closely as Siamese Twins. No government can go alone in this situation. It must take the others with it.

It is fervently hoped that the American society will allow many different cultures to flourish in harmony and that Navajos will be allowed to participate fully through their own enlightened choice.

EPILOGUE

The demographics for the Navajo Nation give an immediate picture of the present and indications of the future. The Navajo Nation is located in the northeastern part of Arizona, the northwestern part of New Mexico, and the southernmost part of Utah.

SIZE	over 24,00 square miles, with limited opportunity for growth of any size.
LANGUAGE	Navajo spoken in 94 percent of homes
ROYALTY INCOME	Oil, gas, and uranium-$84,000,000 a year
PER CAPITA INCOME	Only $2,424 a year
BELOW POVERTY LEVEL	Over 45 percent of the population
UNEMPLOYMENT	Reservation average is 40 percent
MEDIAN AGE	A young 18.8 years
HIGH SCHOOL GRADUATION	A comparable 67 percent of the students
COLLEGE STUDENTS	Only 4,323 students
REGISTERED VOTERS	An amazing 92,622 voters
LIVESTOCK	A whopping 350 percent over the grazing limit
POPULATION:	On reservation 165,000 persons In border towns near reservation 25,000 persons Elsewhere in the United States 25,000 persons
BIRTHRATE	A high 2.7 percent
PROJECTED POPULATION:	By 2015, 360,000 By 2041, 760,000[135]

The U. S. Senate's Special Committee on Investigation of the Select Committee on Indian Affairs, in 1990, recommended that the Bureau of Indian Affairs be gradually eliminated. This recommendation was not

well received by the Navajos or other tribes. One
not familiar with the "love-hate" relationship of the
BIA and Indian tribes would be surprised by this
reaction. First and foremost, the Bureau serves those
Indians on reservations.

Tribal governments have learned how to deal with
the Bureau. The Bureau has Indians in high levels of
administration, proving a sense of comfort to the
tribes. The most avid and vocal groups against the
Bureau are the urban Indians. They constantly work
to get services from the Bureau, but most treaties
and agreements do not cover Indians when they
choose to leave their reservation unless they are a
part of a relocation program. But even under a
relocation program, it stops when the individual
becomes self sufficient.

The Bureau of Indian Affairs is undoubtedly the
least understood branch of the government because of
its legislated ministrations to Indians. There have
been loud outcries from time to time against the
actions of or lack of actions by this agency by
Indian and White alike. However, a special relationship between the Bureau and the Indians does exist.
The following explanation is probably the most realis-
tic one available:

> "The Bureau has been much ma-
> ligned and has made mistakes during
> the many years of its existence.
> However, there is a real feeling on the
> part of the Indian people that it is
> an essential direct contact with the
> federal government that must be main-
> tained.

> The proposal in 1964 to shift the
> education functions of the Bureau
> over to the Office of Education in the
> Department of Health, Education and
> Welfare was resisted violently by
> Indians who saw it as a first step

toward dismantling the Bureau, abro-
gating federal responsibilities and
turning over Indian education to state
education agencies.

Indians can and often do criticize the
Bureau, but they do not necessarily
regard the non-Indian critic as an
ally. They know that criticisms can
play directly into the hands of their
worst enemies--those who wish to
end the special relationship which
exists between the Indians and the
Federal Government.

The Indians do not only tolerate the
injustice of the system; he helps
insulate it from scrutiny and criticism, because history has convinced
him that an attack on the Bureau
will lead to the destruction of his
special status as an Indian and to
the death of his people. This fear
takes a particular form--fear of termination."[136]

In recent years many changes have been made in
the operations of the Bureau. Positions have been
filled with Indians and promotions have gone only to
Indians, resulting in a Bureau that is now primarily
operated by Indians. The powerful BIA Superintendent is now an Indian man or woman. The Bureau has
become more responsive to local input when making
budgets and program decisions.

During the Nixon administration, there was a
surge of proposed new directions for the Indians of
the United States. Although the proposed legislation
was not accepted by Congress, some major changes
were made in the Bureau operations. President Nixon's
policy statements supported the concepts of "self-
determination" during the seventies. The Commissioner of Indian Affairs developed new administrative
guidelines, based on the President's stated policies.

The Bureau was directed to: 1) transform the Bureau from a management to a service organization, 2) reaffirm the trust status of Indian lands, 3) change the role of the Area Offices to include greater emphasis on technical services, 4) give tribes the option of taking over any or all of the BIA program functions with the right of retrocession and , 5) continue present Bureau policies relating to urban Indians with an additional emphasis of a strong Indian advocacy role apparent at all stages of the BIA operations.

The policy gave Indian Tribes and communities the right to participate in planning and operating activities that affected their lives from day to day, and provided that the attitude of "the government knows best" was to be eliminated. Indianization of Indian Affairs was to occur. A National Indian Tribal Chairman's Association was created in 1971 at Pierre, South Dakota. A fifteen man watchdog committee was created to deal with the BIA and Interior officials. In 1972, the Navajo Tribe was one of the first to begin discussions that have led to more and more control of their programs.

Employment assistance training programs were directed into the reservation economies instead of dissipating them in the non-Indian communities. Indians were trained on the reservation for work that was available in their home area, not just in the cities.

Tribal leaders have traditionally fought any programs proposed by the B.I.A. for the urban Indians because they do not want their funds diluted. A solution still has not been found for this growing group of people. Indians who choose to live in off-reservation communities are no longer eligible for federal assistance granted those on the reservations because this limitation is a part of the treaty.

The Indians Water Rights Office was established in the BIA in 1972. It reports directly to the Secretary of the Interior. There will be an increasing demand for water to support the cities and industries of the southwest, and the reserved water rights of Indians will not be very popular with other interests.

As various Indian employees of the Bureau of Indian Affairs begin their careers in civil service, they will run into the same problems that white employees have had over the years. They will have to move to different locations and sites to get promotions and higher salaries. When they supervise the affairs of a tribe unrelated to their tribe, they will become the "BIA Bureaucrat" in the eyes of the local Indians. They will be perceived as someone who does not recognize the local problems, speak the language, or understand the cultural needs.

The time has come to consider more effective ways to handle new problems as they arise. One concept that rarely receives an objective exploration is that there are probably some services and programs that should be administered by the Navajo Tribal Council and some that should be administered by the BIA. Others can be more effectively administered by the states in which the reservations are located. Those programs that are national in nature and involve Indians on a federal level should most certainly be administered by the Bureau. Distribution, monitoring and auditing of federal money designated for the use of Indians should be under the jurisdiction of the Bureau. The preservation and development of Indian lands is a Bureau responsibility. Present scandals involving the misuse of funds and the ability of companies to get permission through BIA officials for these questionable activities may force additional external monitoring of finances within the Department of Interior and the Bureau.

Perhaps in the near future Indian people will be appointed to higher federal offices. The selection of the Secretary of Interior from a part of the country that knows Navajos and their problems was a step in the right direction. The first was Stewart Udall, a member of a pioneer family in Arizona and brother to a popular Arizona congressman, Morris Udall. The second Secretary, Manuel Lujan Jr. was born in San Ildefonso, a small Indian pueblo 18 miles north of Sante Fe, New Mexico. He was the first Republican Congressman elected from New Mexico since 1928. During his term as Secretary of Interior he expressed the belief that the bureau has problems but that they could be remedied.[137]

The newest appointee is Bruce Babbitt, a son of one of the pioneer families in northern Arizona. His family has many reservation business interests. He is a past Attorney General and past Governor of Arizona. With his background he should understand and be able to cope with some of the present problems of the Navajos.

The reservation concept, formulated in the eighteenth century as a way to isolate Indians from the world of the white man, is no longer feasible. The attempts by the government to eliminate reservations has been disastrous to the individual Indians and yet the continued presence of the reservation will cause great problems for the United States Government, the Navajo people and the non-Indians of various states in years to come. The Navajo future will be controlled by the fact that their livestock is 350 percent more than the grazing lands can support, and their birth rate is one of the highest in the United States. The geographic area of the reservation can not be expanded enough to solve the problem. If a solution is not found, there will be great pockets of Navajo Indians living in abject poverty, supported by federal welfare assistance, on the reservation. This situation will eliminate all possibility for self-determination, self-advancement or self-identity for those people.

APPENDIX A

THE EMERGENCE OF A PEOPLE

The events that are contained in this appendix came from several religious ceremonies of the Navajo. They are presented as sequential historical events that tell the religious beginnings and the emergence of the people. These events are not presented sequentially in ceremonies.

The beliefs are still very important to the Navajo to this day. This importance is expressed well in the following passage:

> "To this day, then, the Navajo creation story gives individual Navajos(including many illiterate ones) an important ethnic identity. It defines meaningful relationships among the members of the community and between the community and the entire cosmos."[138]

The main events in the Blessingway are: the emergence, the activities after emergence, the formation of the sacred mountains, the home, the separation of the sexes, the birth of Changing Woman, the puberty rite, conception of the twins, the twins return to their father, Changing Woman's departure to the west, creation of the clans, the mating of corn, the separation of the people and other minor motifs.

The rites for killing and war are in the Monsterway and the Enemyway, two different ceremonies. Monsterway activities are: the birth of the monsters, the childhood of the twins, the journey to meet their father, tests given by their father, the slaying of the monsters, the return to their father and the return home. Enemyway contains the events of: The witch father-in-law of Monster Slayer, the Pueblo Wars, and the ceremonial for Monster Slayer's illness.[139]

Pre-Emergence Events

In the first world, there were beings who were on a small floating mass in a sea of water mist. These beings were of a misty indefinite shape and were not as they are now. Four columns of light, white, blue, yellow, and black, were present. The eastern light was Folding Dawn, the southern light was Folding Sky Blue, the western light was Folding Twilight, and the northern light was Folding Darkness.

Beings in the first world were spider ants, wasps, black ants, beetles, dragon flies, and spiders. There were bats and some holy people. They could make and carry out plans together and knew the secret of witchcraft. First Man was formed from a white and black cloud that met in the east. The first perfect white corn was formed with the kernels covering the whole ear of corn. First Man represented dawn and the giver of life. He used a large, glowing crystal for fire. First Woman was formed when a yellow and blue cloud came together on the west side of this world. A perfect ear of yellow corn was also made. She was given white shell and turquoise. First Woman represented darkness and death. She used turquoise for fire. She noticed the brighter glow of First Man's fire and went to join him. First Man and First Woman had an understanding of what caused good things to happen. But they could not separate good from evil, so they used them both. When there was a lack of harmony, they used good or evil as needed to solve the problem. The Holy Ones encouraged them to do good things.

Coyote traveled to each of the four columns in the misty world. He discovered that witchcraft had been used to create conflict among the beings. The conflict from witchcraft was so great that the beings decided to go to another world. They gathered soil from each of the four sacred mountains. First Man gathered the colored lights and rolled them into small balls so that he could take them. Evil was also taken by the beings to the next world. They floated upward in a spiraling motion to the new world in the east.

The new world contained caves or chambers. Wolves were in white caves of the east. Wildcats lived in the blue caves of the south. Kit foxes had their home in the yellow caves of the west. The black northern caves were home to the mountain lions. There were blue birds, blue hawks, blue jays, blue herons, other blue feathered beings, locusts and crickets.

First Man had Tobacco Worm blow smoke onto the four balls of light to set up the new pillars of light. He brought from below the mountain soil which contained the four mountains and the holy ones that belonged in each one. When Coyote explored this world he found out that the beings fought among themselves because they had different shapes and homes which caused great suffering.

First Man prepared to leave this world. He removed the evil from the insect beings of the first world by blowing smoke in the four directions. He created streaked, zigzag lightning to the east followed by a streak of straight lightening, a rainbow and a sun ray. The beings could not rise to the next world. First Man repeated the activity to the south, west, and north. There was some movement, but not enough to allow them to move into the next world.

Finally, First Man made a wand of jet, turquoise, abalone and white shell with four footprints on it. The beings stood on the footprints and soared through an opening in the southern sky to the new world. The Bluebird led the way followed by First Man, First Woman, Coyote and then the others.

This world was yellow but without a sun. A

female river flowed from north to south. A male river
flowed east to west. There were six mountains in this
world: Dawn or White Shell Mountain to the east;
Blue Bead or Turquoise Mountain to the south;
Abalone Shell Mountain to the west; Obsidian Mountain
to the north; Banded Rock Mountain was in the center; and Many Jewels Mountain was east of Banded
Rock. Turquoise Boy lived beyond White Shell Mountain and White Shell Woman lived in Abalone Shell
Mountain. In this world there were squirrels, chip-
munks, mice, turkeys, foxes, deer cat, spiders, lizards
and snakes.

Coyote talked First Man out of a piece of white
shell. He used it at the water's edge to make the
water go down. After he raised and lowered the
water four times, he found the Water Monster's baby.
He took the baby and hid it under his leg. Water
Monster became angry over the loss of her baby and
caused heavy rains to fall all over the new world.

The birds told First Man that the water was
rising and flooding the land. First Man called all of
the beings to the White Shell Mountain. He planted a
cedar tree but it was too short and the water continued to rise higher and higher up the mountain.

The beings climbed higher up the mountain. First
Man then planted a pine tree and it was too short. A
male reed was also too short. When First Man planted
a female reed it grew and grew to the top of the sky.
The beings went inside the large female reed and
climbed up toward a new world. As they climbed, the
water followed them to the very top of the reed.

They noticed that Coyote was hiding something.
The people searched him and found the water baby.
When they realized that Coyote had caused the flood
by stealing the water baby they became very angry.
Coyote blamed First Woman and told the beings that
she had sent him to steal the water baby. They
ordered Coyote to take the baby to the water's edge
and Water Monster came up for her baby. The beings

gave the mother precious stones with the baby and the water receded back into the lower world.

The locust climbed out of the reed into the new world, which was covered with shining water that glittered. There were monsters in this new world who told Locust that he could not enter unless he could pass certain tests. The first test was for him to sit in the same position for four days without moving. Locust shed his skin and went back into the reed and told the beings what had happened. After four days he returned and the monsters were convinced that he had met the test. The next test was to pass an arrow through his mouth and out the opposite end of his body. The locust did this with ease and the monsters gave the beings permission to enter this new glittering world.[140]

Post Emergence Events

After the beings emerged into the glittering world, First Man and First Woman shaped the four sacred mountains using the mountain soil from the lower worlds. The first mountain was placed in the east. A blanket of white shell was placed on the ground and covered with mountain soil. The mountain soil was then covered with pieces of white shell. They fastened the mountain to the earth with a bolt of white lightning and spread a blanket of daylight decorated with male rain and black clouds over it. Dawn Boy entered this mountain which was guarded by the bear. The mountain was named *Sis naajiní,* White Shell Mountain. We call it Blanca Peak. It lies in Colorado.

The south mountain was made by placing a layer of turquoise on the earth covered by mountain soil with pieces of turquoise over the soil. The mountain was fastened to the earth with a stone knife. A blanket of blue clouds decorated with dart mists and female rain was spread over it. Turquoise Girl entered this mountain which was guarded by Big Snake. This mountain was named *Tsoodził,* Blue Bead or

Turquoise Mountain. We call it Mount Taylor. It is in
New Mexico.

   The western mountain was shaped by placing a
layer of abalone shell on the ground covered by
mountain soil and topped with abalone shell pieces.
It was fastened to the earth by a sunbeam and
covered by a yellow cloud decorated with black
clouds and female rain. Abalone Boy entered this
mountain, which was guarded by the Black Wind. It
was named **dook'o'ooshid,** Abalone Shell Mountain. We
call it Mount Humphreys, highest of the San Francisco
Peaks, in Arizona.

   The northern mountain was made by placing obsidian on the earth covered with mountain soil and
topped off with obsidian pieces. It was covered with
a blanket of darkness decorated with obsidian. Obsidian Girl entered this mountain, which was guarded
by Lightening. It was named **Dibé Nitsaa,** Obsidian
Mountain. We call it Hesperus Peak, of the La Plata
Mountains in Colorado.[141]

   Talking God gave directions for building houses in
the new world. The first two logs were to come from
the east and the west. The next two logs were to be
from the north and the south. A fifth log was to
come from the northeast. All four sides of the house
were to be blessed. A white shell was placed under
the eastern log. Turquoise was placed under the
southern log. Abalone shell was placed under the
western log, and obsidian under the northern log.
All four objects were placed under the fifth log.
Bird feathers were attached to the top of the roof
where all of the logs came together. Pollen was
placed underneath the top of the house. White
cornmeal, yellow cornmeal and pollen were used to
bless the house. The door was to be placed facing
the east because all prayers and songs start with the
east. This house was called **alch'į'adeez'í,** male house
and it had a vestibule. The male house was to be
used for ceremonial gatherings, religious matters, and
eating. Uneaten food was to be removed after meals.

The *Hooghan Nímazí,* female house was placed south of the male house. It was more round and did not have a vestibule. This was where women could talk, men could laugh and tell stories and children could laugh and play.[142]

ILLUSTRATION 8:   THE MALE HOUSE

The beings realized that the light in this world was as dim as it had been in the lower worlds. They needed a brighter light. Beings were dying and no one knew what to do with them. Coyote decided that the way to solve the problem was to devise a test. He would take a black rock to Black Water Lake and throw it in. If it floated, the spirits of the dead would come up there and no one would die. If the rock sank, the spirits of the dead would return to the lower worlds. Coyote threw the rock into the lake and it sank, so now the spirits of the dead go to the lower world.

ILLUSTRATION 9: THE FEMALE HOUSE

It was decided by the beings that they wanted
neither light nor dark all of the time. So they divided time into day and night. They wanted stars in
the night sky. They selected the stars they wanted
and placed them on a blanket. First Man placed the
Big Dipper in the sky and First Woman placed the
Little Dipper. First Man placed the seven stars that
represent the parts of the body. Next the main stars
were placed and instructed to guard and protect the
sky and beings.

Coyote trotted by and asked what they were
doing. When they told him, he asked to help. He
placed a star in the south and said that this was to
be the morning star. Coyote soon became bored with
this orderly process so he grabbed the corners of
the blanket and tossed the remaining stars into the
sky.   First Man became very angry, but Coyote was
pleased with himself.

First Man and First Woman decided that there should be a sun for the day time and a moon for the night time. They spread six special buckskins on the ground. The buckskins had not been pierced by an arrow or knife and there was no scar on them. They placed a large round turquoise on the buckskins and painted a face with a mouth, a nose and eyes with a yellow streak below the mouth. Six additional special buckskins were placed on top of the turquoise to make the sun.

Next a large perfect white shell was placed on a buckskin to make the moon. It was decided that the sun and moon would move from east to west so their light would shine all over the world.

Someone had to carry the sun and the moon. A sun carrier was selected first. Then the moon carrier. The carriers decided that there must be a penalty paid for carrying the sun and the moon. This price was that beings would die every day and night.

One Walking Giant came to the beings and asked them to play the Moccasin Game with him at the house made of banded rock. The beings did not know the game and they refused. He came twice more and asked them to play, but each time they refused. A flying messenger warned the beings to play the giant at Red Rock on the eastern side of the Lukachukai Mountains. They were not to play at the house made of banded rock. When the giant returned for the fourth time, the beings agreed to play the Moccasin Game at Red Rock. The Holy People came to watch.

The giant came on the fourth day and explained the game. There were 102 markers made from the yucca plant and a small ball made from the inside of the Yucca plant. The markers were to keep track of the points earned. Four moccasins were placed side by side on the ground. The beings who were awake in the daytime were to line up on one side of the moccasins and the night beings on the other. One side would secretly hide the ball in a moccasin. The opposite side used a stick to tap the moccasin which they thought contained the hidden ball.

If someone thought that the ball was in a moccasin it was tapped once. If they thought the ball was not in that moccasin, it was to be tapped more than once. If one side stated that the ball was in a moccasin and it was, it was taken out and given to them to hide in the moccasins for their side. When players guessed that the ball was not in the moccasin, and it was, they were penalized. They had to pay 10 markers to the other side who kept the ball. The game continued until one side had won all of the markers.

The giant explained that the losers of the game had to pay a penalty. If the night beings won, it would always be night time. If the day beings won, it would always be day time. The giant darkened one side of a corn husk and threw it into the air. The unmarked side of the corn husk was up so the day beings began the game. They played all night and neither side could win all of the markers. The night beings were getting nervous because they knew that the sun was coming up and they wanted to be home before daylight. So they called the game a draw and that is why each day has daylight and darkness.[143]

The beings now had stars, a sun by day and a moon by night. They decided that the year should be divided into seasons. First Man and First Woman decided that spring would be the season for planting things. Growing things would mature during summer. When the plants were mature and needed to be harvested, it was to be fall. When the growing things had been harvested, it would become winter time. The lightning would wake everyone when winter was over and the spring season would begin again. Lightning was also to be a warning for beings so that they would not tell certain stories at the wrong time of the year. These stories were to be told only after the last rains and only until the first lightning of spring.

It was planting time for growing things. First Man supplied white corn seeds and First Woman supplied yellow corn seeds. Turkey supplied gray, blue, black and red corn seeds. Big Snake supplied pumpkin, watermelon, cantaloupe and muskmelon seeds. The crops grew and the first harvest was very good. The beings now had daylight and darkness, a place for the dead, the seasons and a good harvest, so every thing was very good.[144]

The Separation of The Sexes

First Woman and Turquoise Boy committed adultery. When First Man heard of the event, he was very hurt and upset about it. He stayed inside his house and did not tell the leaders what they were to do each day. Others began to commit adultery and the practice grew. First Man summoned the Hermaphrodite and asked if it could cook, do the weaving and fix the men's hair. The Hermaphrodite agreed to do these tasks. First Man and those men who did not commit adultery decided to leave the women.

They built a raft and crossed the river where two waters flowed together. The water was swift and it was a dangerous crossing. First Man left the men who practiced adultery with the women because they wanted to stay with the women.

The women laughed and mocked the men. They said that they could do without men and would not need them. The men that were left behind soon became physically exhausted and their strong desires disappeared. They changed physically. The men across the river did not suffer for they had the Hermaphrodite to do the cooking and other chores.

Some women drowned when they tried to cross the river to the men. The rest of them became lazy and did not tend the crops. They used strange objects and animals to satisfy their sexual desires. New

giants and monsters were born. Finally the women
called to the men and asked to live with them again.
The men did not want all of the women to die. They
returned and performed the proper rituals and puri-
fications so that men and women could live together
again.[145]

The beings then became more human in appearance, but the Holy Ones remained as spirits. The
people increased in number and there were good
crops.

The Monsters

Monsters that were created when the sexes were
apart not only frightened people but killed and ate
them. It was not safe anywhere. . Big Monster lived
on top of Mount Taylor. He killed people with clubs
of black, blue and multicolor flint and then ate them.
Horned Monster roamed everywhere. He had good
eyesight and a horn. When people came near he
would run over them and then kill them with his
horn. A family of bird monsters with a husband, a
wife and two children, lived on top of Shiprock. The
parents flew over the land picking up people and
dropping them to their deaths in the nest to feed the
children. Monster That Kicked People Off the Cliff
sat against Kicking Rock on the trail and kicked
people over the edge of the cliff. The monster's
children ate the victims. Monster That Killed With His
Eyes hypnotized his victims and then ate them.
There were other monsters in different places such as
Rolling Rock, Moving Sand, Tracking Bear and
others.[146]

Changing Woman

First Man and First Woman had been told that
when there were enough people, Changing Woman
would be born. One morning First Man noticed a
cloud on top of Gobernado Knob. He climbed to the
top of the mountain to investigate and found a little
baby girl. The baby was born of darkness with dawn

as her father. The Holy Ones gave First Man and First Woman directions for raising the baby. The Holy Ones performed a special ceremony for her when she reached puberty This ceremony was called Walks in Beauty and is performed for girls to this day when they reach puberty.

First Woman spread out a perfect buckskin and placed a piece of turquoise, abalone, obsidian and white shell on it. She dressed the girl in white moccasins with leggings and a skirt of white beads. The blouse sleeve fringes and wristlets were also of white beads. She placed white shell beads, turquoise beads, abalone beads and obsidian beads around the girl's neck. She also gave the girl earrings.

Talking God spread out a white buckskin covered by a clear doeskin, a white cotton fabric, a woven fabric and finally a white robe. The girl lay face down on the materials with her head to the east, arms outstretched and her legs spread outwards. Talking God used his hands to mold her body from her forehead down to her hips. Then he shaped her body from her feet up to her forehead. He rubbed her body with pollen gathered at dawn, twilight and after darkness. Next the girl was directed to run four times toward the rising sun turning sunwise to return. These events were performed each day for three days.

Every day before the girl ran, she picked up each fabric and made a motion in the four directions. She moved the white robe from east to west, the clear doeskin and the white buckskin were moved over the earth's surface. As she made motions with the materials she said, "This will be found everywhere."

An offering was made to the sun and the moon. Girls now bake corn meal cakes for this purpose. When the ceremonies were completed, the girl was named "Changing Woman." She is sometimes called White Shell Woman because of the white shells on her clothes. [147]

When Changing Woman was grown, she took a bath
at a small waterfall. She lay down to dry and fell
asleep. She was impregnated by the sun while she
slept. When she awakened she let the water run over
her. In time, she had twin boys. As they grew, she
gave them her love and had them exercise daily so
they would be strong. They wrestled and ran to the
top of the mountain each morning. When there was
snow on the ground they rolled in it naked so that
they would become strong.[148]

The Journey to The Sun

The monsters roamed everywhere and the people
were frightened because they felt helpless. When
the twins were men, they asked their mother who
their father was, but she would only tell them that he
was very powerful and dangerous.

One day while the twins were hunting, they found
a hole in the ground, the home of Spider Woman.
They entered the hole and found that it was a beautiful home. They told Spider Woman that they wanted
to get help from their father to slay the monsters
that were roaming the earth. She told them that the
sun was their father. Spider Woman also warned
them that the trip to see the sun would be very dangerous.

Spider Woman agreed to help the twins and taught
them things that only she knew. They were fed from
baskets that never became empty. She put a small
piece of turquoise into the corn meal of the older
twin to give him courage and a strong heart. The
gifts of magic eagle feathers and special protection
against poison were the last items given to the twins.
She taught them the correct names, chants and
prayers to be used when encountering all of the
guardians of the sun. When they did meet a guardian, they were to call it by its proper name and sing
the proper chant or prayer to pass in safety.

The twins stayed with Spider Woman a long time

to learn all of the names, chants and prayers. When they were ready, they set out for their father's house in the west. They first arrived at a place where the water flowed out of the ground. The guardian here was Reeds That Cut. The water lured people near and the reeds cut them. These reeds were so sharp that when someone was cut he would bleed to death. There were bones lying all around the water. When the twins called out the correct name and sang the special prayer, the reeds allowed them to drink as much water as they wanted without harming them.

Next they came to Moving Sand where a person would slide down and be buried beneath the sand. The twins called it by its proper name and sang the right prayer. They climbed higher and higher passing many bones on their way up the sand. They climbed over the top and continued safely on their way.

The twins came to Canyon Which Closes in on a Traveler. They called it by its proper name but it closed so fast that they did not have time to sing the proper prayer. They rode out of the canyon on the magic eagle feathers given to them by Spider Woman just as the canyon closed under their feet.

The next place was the Four Pillars of Rock that represent old age. They had to pass on the sunny south side of the pillars or they would die of old age. The twins forgot and started walking on the shady cool trail on the north side of the pillars. Some of their hair became white on the ends as they passed the first pillar. As they passed the second pillar, white streaks developed in their hair. A messenger flew to them and warned them, so they turned and passed the last two pillars on the south side. They then realized that had they passed the last two pillars on the north side, they would have died of old age.

The next guardian was called Wash That Swallows.

The twins called it by the proper name and sang the correct prayer. They found Measuring Worm and rode safely across the wash on his back as they had been instructed to do by Spider Woman.

Finally the twins reached the ocean in the west, where they met the Water Skeeters described by Spider Woman. They agreed to take the twins on beyond a place called Darkness to the home of the sun. On the way the twins met the four doorkeepers of the sun, Gigantic Snake, Huge Black Bear, Big Thunder and Big Wind. They passed safely using the correct names and prayers taught them by Spider Woman.[149]

They were met by the wife of the sun. She was not very happy to find out that her husband had other children. The wife warned them to leave because she was afraid Sun would try to kill them when he returned from carrying the sun disk through the sky. Sun had seen them enter the house from the sky and when he returned, he asked if there were visitors. His wife explained that they were his sons but he was not convinced and decided to test them to see if they really were his sons.

Sun lit a pipe filled with poisoned tobacco and passed it to the twins to smoke. They smoked it to the four directions and told Sun that they felt fine. They used the special protection against poisons that they carried with them and it kept them safe.

Next Sun instructed them to take a sweat bath. Sun's daughter dug a deep hole in the floor of the sweat house and told the twins to hide in it. Sun made the heat so great that it would destroy anyone inside. Each time he asked them how they felt, they would reply that they felt fine. Finally he asked them to come out of the sweat house.

Sun gave the twins cornmeal that contained a poison. Their protection against poisons saved them again. Sun next threw the twins against sharp flint

knives, but the twins used their magic eagle feathers
and were not injured.

Sun then realized that these young men must
truly be his sons and asked his daughter to bathe
them. She washed them in a white bead basket, a
turquoise basket, a white shell basket and finally in
an obsidian basket. He molded the twins' arms, legs,
fingers, faces and bodies, shaping them into very
handsome young men. Their father then dressed
them in beautiful clothes.

Sun showed them his house and told them they
could have anything that they wanted. In the east
room were the finest seeds of corn and other plants.
Wild animals were in the south room. Domesticated
animals including the horse were in the west room.
There were precious jewels in the north room.

The twins explained that they needed something
that would help them kill the monsters so their people
could be safe. Sun was reluctant to help the twins
because some monsters were his children. Eventually
he agreed to help the twins. Sun gave them lightning that looked like bows and arrows. He gave the
older twin dark flint armor and gave blue flint armor
to the younger twin. The sun named the older twin
Monster Slayer and the younger son Child Born of
Water.

Monster Slayer's weapon was called Lightning That
Flashes Crooked. Child Born of Water's weapon was
called Lightning That Flashes Straight. Sun warned
them that Big Monster had four lightning arrows that
the twins must steal to defeat him. Sun asked for
the tail feather from the headdress of big Monster as
his reward. He then returned the twins to a place
called Hot Springs.[150]

The Slaying of The Monsters

Big Monster lived near Hot Springs. The twins
waited beside a lake for him to come for a drink of

water. Soon the monster came to drink and saw the twins.

He asked them how he should kill them, but the twins asked him how he wanted them to kill him. They called back and forth four times. Four times the monster tried to shoot the twins with lightning arrows, but they rode their magic eagle feathers and he missed them each time. The twins shot the monster with a blinding flash of lightning but still he stood. They used all of their weapons until at last he fell. The ground shook when the monster fell and his blood began to flow out on the ground. A messenger flew to warn the twins not to let the monster's blood come together on the ground or he would rise again. The twins kept the streams of blood separated and the monster died.

Monster Slayer collected the tail feather from the monster's headdress for his father. The twins left the lake and went to the home of their mother. She did not believe that they had killed Big Monster until they showed her its dried blood. This dried blood is now believed by non-Navajos to be a lava bed near Grants, New Mexico.

Monster Slayer went to a place called Wild Horse Mesa near Mesa Verde to find Monster That Kicks People Off the Cliff. He found the monster and pretended to step in front of him on the trail. As the monster kicked at him, he jumped back and killed the monster with his flint knife. He tried to throw him over the cliff, but the monster's hair had grown into the rock. Monster Slayer had to cut the hair before he could throw the monster over the cliff.

Monster Slayer told Child Born of the Water to stay home and keep a torch burning. He was to blow smoke to the four directions while Monster Slayer was trying to kill Horned Monster. Monster Slayer located Horned Monster but could not get close enough to kill him because of his long horn. The monster's thick hair looked like that of a moose.

ILLUSTRATION 10:   MONSTER SLAYER AND CHILD OF THE WATER

The Monster Slayer

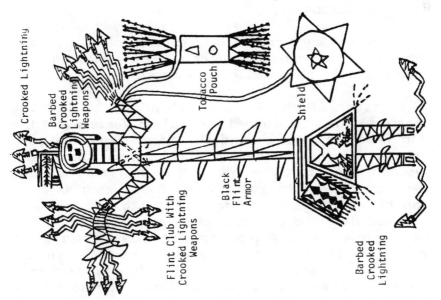

Child of the Water

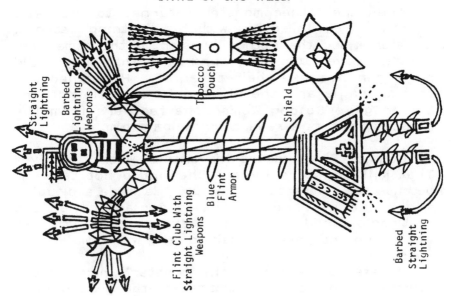

Gopher agreed to help Monster Slayer and dug a tunnel directly below the heart of Horned Monster. Gopher chewed off the hair over the heart of Horned Monster so that Monster Slayer could kill him with his lightning weapons.

Monster Slayer returned home and told his mother about slaying Horned Monster. She would not believe him until he produced the monster's skin.

Monster Slayer went to Shiprock to kill the Monster Birds. He carried some blood vessels and the skin from the monster and the magic eagle feathers. Monster Bird saw Monster Slayer from above and swooped down to catch him in his claws. The monster's skin kept Monster Slayer from being injured. Monster Bird carried him high into the air and dropped him into the nest of young monsters. The magic eagle feathers kept Monster Slayer from being injured by the fall. He broke open the blood vessels so that it appeared that he was bloody and dead from the fall. When the young monsters approached, he scared them off, telling them that if they were quiet, he would not kill them.

When the father monster returned to the nest, Monster Slayer killed him with his lightning weapons. He later killed the mother monster in the same way. Monster Slayer told the young ones that they could no longer live like their parents. He turned one into an eagle and the other into an owl. Monster Slayer gave Spider Woman the feathers from the monster birds as a reward for helping him.

Monster Slayer asked his mother where the Eyes That Kill Monsters lived. She would not tell him because they were so dangerous. He made a cloud of smoke and watched it drift to a place called the Continental Divide. Monster Slayer visited with Salt Woman and she gave him salt to take with him.

Monster Slayer found the monster's home at the Continental Divide. He dropped to the ground when the monsters came out of their house to see if anyone was near. When they returned to the house he ran closer. Four times the monsters came out and each time Monster Slayer got closer to the house. When he looked inside the house the monsters were sitting around an open fire. He threw the salt on the flames and it exploded, blinding the monsters. Monster Slayer then killed them with a flint club, taking the eyes and scalps home to his mother to prove to her that he had killed the monsters.

Monster Slayer prepared four fire arrows to take with him to find the Running Antelopes who were killing people. He found them resting in the Jemez Mountains. He shot an arrow into the east and when it hit the ground it caused a great column of smoke. The antelopes ran to the spot and poked about with their horns. When they could not find anyone they returned to their resting place. He shot the next arrow to the south. The antelopes ran to the column of smoke and again returned to their resting place.

The antelopes were becoming tired from all of the running. Monster Slayer shot his third arrow to the west causing a great column of smoke. The antelopes ran to the column of smoke and poked around with their horns again. When they returned to their resting place they were very tired. Monster Slayer fired his last arrow to the north. The antelopes ran to this place and found nothing. When they ran back to their resting place they were so tired that they could hardly walk. Monster Slayer sprang from his hiding place and told the antelopes that he was going to kill them because they had been killing people. The antelopes pleaded for their lives. Monster Slayer relented when they agreed to stop killing people and to eat only special grasses. The antelopes then spread out over all of the land and became food for humankind.

Monster Slayer directed Child Born of The Water to wait for him, keeping a torch burning for his safety. If he was in danger the torch would flame

up, warning his brother of that fact. Monster Slayer
found Rolling Rock on the side of Mount Taylor. The
monster was perfectly round and very large. Rolling
Rock began moving toward Monster Slayer slowly.
Monster Slayer's zigzag lightning broke on the monster rock. His flint club did not break it. Rolling
Rock began to move toward him faster and faster.
The flame of the torch held by Child Born of the
Water began to flare. He went searching for his
brother for he knew that Monster Slayer was in
trouble.

When the twins came together they took turns
striking Rolling Rock. One twin would run up one
side and strike the rock and then the other twin
would run up the opposite side and strike the rock.
Rolling Rock felt that he was about to be overcome
and rolled to the west trying to escape.

He went past Hot Springs, past The Place Spotted
With Juniper and on to Jacob's Wells where he
stopped. The twins built a fire on the rock and
placed special herbs in it to heat the rock. When the
rock became very hot, they began striking large
chunks from it with their flint clubs. They finally
split it into four equal parts. They found the heart
inside and took it home to prove that they had slain
Rolling Rock.

The twins were resting after killing the monsters
when they saw a red glow in the distance. They
became curious and went to a place where they found
smoke coming from a hole in the ground. The twins
saw old looking people resting in a room. They found
a doorway and entered the room where these beings
were sleeping. They decided that they were probably
monsters and set out to kill them.

The first one they approached said that he was
"hunger" and the people could not live without him in
the future. People were born with the need to eat
food and if they did not have hunger, they would not
eat. The twins spared his life and moved on to

another being. The next being pleaded with them not
to kill him because he was "poverty." While he lived,
clothing would wear out and people would have needs.
He was allowed to live.

They raised their clubs to kill the next being
when he opened his eyes and told them that he was
"sleep" and they should not kill him. People needed
to sleep when they were ill or tired. Sleep restored
energy to people. They let him live. The next being
told them that he was "lice" and that he kept people
clean. If people were not clean, lice got into their
hair. He was allowed to remain.

The last being watched them approach then told
them that he was "old age." If he was killed, no one
would get old and die. There would be too many
people and the young ones would not be born. They
let him live and returned to their home.

The twins then traveled to each of the four
sacred mountains and surveyed the land for monsters.
They found no monsters anywhere. They returned
their weapons to their father because they had no
further use for them.

This time Sun greeted them with friendliness and
asked them the purpose of their visit. The twins told
him and explained that they would like to have some
of the treasures from his house. At first Sun was reluctant because he had made a great sacrifice the
first time they were there by helping them kill some
of his monster children. He finally said that if they
wanted something this time they would have to give
him something in return. The twins agreed to help
Sun kill some of his enemies when they returned
home.

The twins received many gifts from the rooms in
their father's house including obsidian, turquoise,
white shell, and abalone shell horses from the room in
the east. They received elk, antelope, porcupine,
deer, and rabbit from the south room. Seeds of

white, blue, yellow, black and variegated corn with
pollen came from the room in the west. They received plants and small birds from the room in the
north. They returned home with all these fine gifts
from their father.[151]

The Squaw Dance

One night Monster Slayer saw a fire in the distance. When he went to that spot in the morning, he
could find nothing. On the fourth morning, he found
a house and entered it. The house was carpeted with
fabrics and had strands of beads, perfect shell discs
and earrings hanging on the wall, and a beautiful
maiden was there.

A jovial old man entered the house and acted
very happy. He asked Monster Slayer to smoke with
him. They took out their pipes and tobacco pouches
and placed them on the floor. Monster Slayer saw
that the pipes and pouches were identical. A messenger whispered to Monster Slayer that the old man
used witchcraft and killed with his tobacco. The old
man mixed up the pipes and tobacco pouches and held
them out to Monster Slayer. A messenger told Monster Slayer which ones to choose. They smoked and
the old man asked to smoke Monster Slayer's pipe.
He filled it with tobacco and gave it to the old man.
When the old man inhaled a large puff of smoke, he
fell over and appeared dead. The girl called her
mother who begged Monster Slayer to restore her
husband. This happened four times before the old
man could smoke the pipe.

The old man asked Monster Slayer to stay with
his daughter. When the old man left, the daughter
spread blankets for Monster Slayer with his head to
the north. The messenger warned Monster Slayer to
move the blankets with his head to the east. The
messenger warned him not to have any sexual relations with the girl. The girl tried to get Monster
Slayer to make love to her all night, but he resisted
her advances.

At daylight she brought him food in a basket. The messenger warned Monster Slayer that the food next to him on the basket had been sprinkled with witch powder. Monster Slayer turned the basket and ate from the opposite side. When the girl went out-side, the old man asked her how he ate his food. When she told him, he could not understand how Monster Slayer evaded his poison. Monster Slayer went to Blanca Peak and killed a buck and ate part of it.

That night the messenger again warned Monster Slayer not to have anything to do with the girl. At daylight she brought food to him. The messenger told Monster Slayer that the poison was on the out-side edge of the basket, so he ate from the part closest to him. News of his continued health puzzled the old man even more. Monster Slayer went to Mount Taylor where he killed a buck and ate part of the meat.

On the third night the same events took place. When food was brought at daylight, the messenger told Monster Slayer that the poison was all around the outside edge of the basket, so he ate from the center. The old man decided that he was not dealing with an ordinary man. Monster Slayer went to the San Francisco Peaks and killed a buck, eating part of the meat.

The messenger told Monster Slayer that he could make love to the maid on the fourth night. When the food was brought at daylight, the messenger told him that the witch powder was all over the food. Monster Slayer told the girl that he would not eat that day. The old man was furious and left the house in a rage. The girl then told Monster Slayer that her father was a witch, and that every time a young man came to her he was killed by her father's witchcraft.

Monster Slayer went to Hesperus Peak and killed a buck. This time he brought the meat home. He told his wife that they would only eat deer meat and taught her how to make jerky and how to tan the hide of the deer.

When Monster Slayer went hunting, the old man took beautiful things from the house. The wife of Monster Slayer told him that her father knew the Enemyway and that was what made him powerful. He used this ceremony to make war upon his enemies and to witch people in his home. All of the treasures in the house were from maidens killed by the old man. She knew the songs and chants and wanted to teach them to Monster Slayer. He said that he would think about it.

Monster Slayer and his wife did not share their deer meat with the old man and his wife. The old man set about trying to kill Monster Slayer with his witchcraft. He took Monster Slayer to a place where he had made tracks that looked like those of a big buck leading into a box canyon. While Monster Slayer followed the tracks into the canyon, the old man changed himself into a big snake. He waited for Monster Slayer to come back out of the canyon. The messenger warned Monster Slayer and told him to grab the old man by the glottis in his throat. When this happened, the old man changed himself back to a man and they went home, going their separate ways.

Monster Slayer's wife heard about this and became frightened so she made a medicine bag out of deer skin like the one her father used for his medicine. She dyed it yellow like his but left out important medicines. Then she switched the bags giving her father's strong medicine to her husband. She then taught him the chants and prayers of Enemyway. The old man could kill no more because he no longer had his powerful medicine bag. Being powerless, he could cause no harm to Monster Slayer.

Monster Slayer used the power of Enemyway to organize a war against the Pueblo people. He forgot to tell Talking God but he caught up with the war party and helped them plan the raid. They killed all of the people, taking their scalps and other items of value.

Soon after this war, Monster Slayer became ill. Blood and the smell of the monsters he killed were making him ill. The blood from the scalps of the Pueblos that he had killed was also making him ill. The Holy Ones organized a group sing for Monster Slayer to cure him. This was the very first Squaw Dance and it is still performed for those who are ill or going to face danger.[152]

Formation of The Clans

Changing Woman moved to a home that the Sun built for her in the ocean to the west. She took several beings with her so that she would not be lonesome. The beings eventually became homesick and wanted to return.

Changing Woman decided it was time to have humans so she rubbed some skin from under her breast and formed **kiyaa'áanii**, the Towering House Clan. She rubbed some skin from her back and formed **honágháahnii**, the One Walks Around You Clan. She formed **tó dísh' nii**, the Bitter Water Clan from skin under her right arm. **hashtł' ishnii**, the Mud Clan was formed from skin under her left arm.

Changing Woman also appointed an animal guardian to each clan. The bear was to guard the Towering House Clan. The lion was named for the One Walks Around You Clan. The bull snake was named to the Bitter Water Clan and the porcupine went to the Mud Clan.

The animal guardians and humans were transported by sunbeams to Bill Williams' Mountain. Talking God and Second Talking God made sacrifices of precious stones on the top of the San Francisco Peaks. The group continued their journey to the old homelands of the beings.

When they came to Female Mountain, they found a
corn plant. The plant had white corn at the top and
yellow corn at the bottom. They placed the corn
plant on a piece of black cotton material and covered
it with a piece of white cotton material. They then
said a chant. Two men and two women rose from the
ground and joined the people on their journey.

When they arrived at the Corner of Mountain they
found a large vacant house. There were magic quiv-
ers for arrows hanging on the walls. The inhabitants
were called Many Arrows People and attacked the
people at Black Mountain. They would have been
killed if it had not been for the animal guardians
given to them by Changing Woman. They helped
defeat the Many Arrows People.

They journeyed past Water On It and came to
Tuba City. The people were very thirsty and one of
them stuck a white shell cane into the ground and
water came out. At the east side of Black Mountain
another person stuck a turquoise cane into the
ground and water came up out of the ground. At
Tonalea they found two pillars of rock. The person
carrying the obsidian cane stuck it into the ground
and muddy water came out of the ground. To this
day there is still a muddy hole at Tonalea.

As the people moved on, they released their
animal guardians. The bear had been left at Water on
It to be a rear guard. The lion was released on the
east side of Black Mountain and the bull snake was
released at Mountainous Region. When they arrived
at Beautiful Mountain the porcupine was released.
Under the protection and guidance of the Holy Ones,
more clans were created as the people went on to
their old homelands. [153]

The Blessingway

Changing Woman took two boys from their homes
to learn the Blessingway. She explained that the
people the boys lived with had left for the east

before learning the necessary songs and prayers and could not bless their homes. They had no special ceremonies. The boys were to learn the Blessingway songs and prayers. This would make them strong when traveling and healthy in body and spirit. These songs and prayers would make their thoughts and speech holy so they would get to know the Holy Ones.

The first night was spent in the east room of dawn. The boys were told how the earth was made, as well as the sky, dawn, horizontal blue, evening twilight, darkness, the sun and the moon. They learned all of the proper names, songs and prayers for these things. They were taught the major home songs so that they could live securely and their homes would be holy.

The next night was spent in the south room of horizontal blue. The same things were presented again. The boys were told how the mountains were made and decorated. They were told about the spirits in the mountains. Changing Woman taught them the songs and prayers for the sacred mountains of Blanca Peak, Mount Taylor, Hesperus Peak and the San Francisco Peaks. She also taught them about Huerfano Mountain and Gobernado Knob.

The third evening's activities were in the west room of evening twilight. Changing Woman told the boys how she had made the people in the west. They learned the songs that told how Changing Woman was born, about her life and her puberty ceremony. They learned about the twins, their trip to their father, and how the monsters were destroyed. These songs are a part of Monsterway.

As Changing Woman walked around in the different rooms she appeared to change in age. When she was in the south, she became a middle aged woman. When she was in the west, she became an old woman. As she moved from room to room, she changed in age from young to old and then to young. She explained that this was why she was called Changing Woman.

The fourth night was spent in the north room of darkness. The boys were told that when someone had nightmares, perfect ears of corn should be used in the ceremony to cure the nightmares. Then Changing Woman brought them into her room and bathed them with dew and dried them with pollen. The Holy Ones came to the house and helped the boys memorize all of the songs and prayers. The boys were told to teach all of their people the Blessingway and the other songs that they had learned from Changing Woman. She then sent them home on sun rays.

The Holy Ones called all of the people together to develop mountain soil bundles. It was explained that the mountain soil bundles must be made before the people could be taught the Blessingway.

The Holy Ones instructed the different clans to go to the tops of the sacred mountains. The Bitter Water Clan sent a fast runner carrying a prayer stick of white shell with a feather on it, to the top of Blanca Peak. The Water is Close Clan sent their runner to the top of Mount Taylor carrying a tur- quoise prayer stick with a feather on it. Towering House Clan's runner carried a prayer stick of abalone shell with a feather on it to the top of the San Francisco Peaks. The Mud Clan runner carried a jet prayer stick to the top of Hesperus Peaks. The runners also took white shell, turquoise, abalone shell and jet for sacrifices.

Women were taught how to make baskets. The Holy Ones told them that no more than four baskets could ever be used for ceremonies. The men built a large house while the baskets were being made. The run- ners then gathered soil from the east side of each mountain and brought back the dew from the feathers and put it in the baskets containing the soil. Talking God gave them an unblemished white buckskin. The Holy Ones explained that only the unblemished skin from an animal killed by tying its snout and inserting pollen into the nostrils could be used for making the mountain soil bags. The buckskin that was left over should be reverently made into something useful.

Talking God asked for a choice ear of white corn, blue corn and speckled corn, which are male. He asked for a choice ear of yellow corn, gray, and striped corn, which are female. Fabrics, jewels, pollens and dews were also gathered. The twelve materials were then placed into the baskets.

A piece of buckskin was cut from the left foreleg and the soil from Blanca Peak was placed on it. A piece of buckskin cut from the left rear leg was used for the soil from the San Francisco Peaks. Buckskin cut from the right foreleg was used for the soil from Hesperus Peak. The soil from Mount Taylor was placed on a piece of buckskin cut from the right foreleg. Soil was also gathered from Gobernado Knob and placed in a piece of buckskin cut from the center of the skin. The soil from Huerfano Mountain was placed in a piece of buckskin cut from the left side of center where the heart was located. Dews, fabrics, jewels and pollens were placed in the pieces of buckskin for Gobernado Knob and Huerfano Mountain.

A choice, perforated white shell bead was placed at the bottom of the soil from Blanca Peak. A strip of buckskin was cut from the tip of the tail to the head from the right side of the spine. The bag was wrapped with this strip in a sunwise motion. A jewel dipped in the mouth of a small blue bird was attached to the east side of the bag.

A choice, perforated turquoise bead was placed at the bottom of the soil from Mount Taylor. A strip of buckskin was cut from the area next to the last cut and the bag was wrapped with it. A jewel dipped in the mouth of a blue swift was attached to the east side of the bag.

An abalone bead was placed at the bottom of the soil from the San Francisco Peaks. The strip of

buckskin was cut next to the last strip and was used
to wrap the bag.   A jewel dipped in the mouth of a
small tanager was attached to the east side of the
bag.

An obsidian bead was placed in the soil from
Hesperus Peak.   The strip of buckskin was cut next
to the last one.   A jewel dipped in the mouth of a
corn beetle was attached to the east side of the bag.

These bags were called Mountain Soil, and to this
day, Blessingway ceremonies cannot be performed
without them.   The Holy Ones explained that if anyone
knew the songs for making the mountain soil, they
could make it and be in harmony with the Holy
People.

The bags of soil from Gobernado Knob and Huerfano Mountain represented the male and female homes
and were added so that all home things would be
strong.   Banded aragonite, white aragonite, fetishes,
transparent rock crystals and game fetishes were to
be carried with the mountain soils.   The mountain
soils would be kept fresh by adding the shaken-off
pollen, small bird shaken-off pollen and rainbow
shaken-off pollen.

Mountain soil bags were placed inside a bag made
of otter skin and tied with strips of buckskin.   The
Holy Ones explained that buckskin could be used
when an otter skin was not available.   Bags of pollen
were made and placed in the baskets made by the
women.   These were all of the things to be used for
the Blessingway ceremonies. [154]

Changing Woman appeared and explained the
various ways the Blessingway could be used and the
way to do it. The people had been with the Holy Ones
for many days and nights when they received the
following message:

"The Holy People announced that
after their departure from that cere-

monial they would never be seen again
and warned people that dire conse-
quences would follow if anyone should
claim that he had seen a holy one.
They said however that their presence
would be made manifest in the sound
of the wind, the feather of an eagle,
in various small birds, or in the
growth of corn."[155]

People then moved all over the lands. One group
moved to the south and became the Chiricahua Apaches. Another group moved to the east and became
the Mescalero Apaches. A third group was left in the
La Plata Mountains and became the Jicarilla Apaches.
The group that was left in the Navajo Mountain area
became the Paiutes.

The land within the boundaries of the four sacred
mountains became home for the people. A Holy One
was left in each of the sacred mountains. One Holy
One, whose body starts at the foot of Mount Taylor,
curves around the outside of the four sacred mountains, with the head stopping at Blanca Peak. This
Holy One protects the people living within its boundary.

Some people now live beyond this
boundary of the four sacred mountains
and they have difficulties with nature
for they are out of harmony with the
plans of the Holy Ones.[156]

The major details of the Blessingway ceremony
and other Holyway ceremonies are described in
several sources. One detailed source is that of
Father Berard Haile. He translated three versions of
the Blessingway, each told a little differently by the
singers. It is edited by Lelan C. Wyman in Blessingway published by the University of Arizona
Press.

Mary Wheelwright details most of the Blessingway in her work titled Navajo Creation Myth,

published by the   Museum of Navajo Ceremonial Art.

Gladys A. Reichard has compiled the most comprehensive   study of the   religion and sand   paintings done by any person   in *Navajo Medicine Man/
Sandpainting*, printed   by Dover Publications, Inc.
and *Navajo Religion, A Study in Symbolism*,   printed
by Princeton University Press. Her studies covered a
25 year period of research   effort.

The work   edited by Ethelou Yazzie called *Navajo
History, Volume I*, published by Navajo Community
College, is an excellent description of the major
religious events in the creation stories of the Navajos.

Paul G. Salbrod emphases the importance of these
beliefs in his publication, *Diné bahané, The Navajo
Creation Story*, published by the University of New
Mexico Press.

APPENDIX B

SOUTHWESTERN INDIAN POPULATIONS-1993

TRIBE | POPULATION

Acoma Pueblo................................1,365
Cochiti Pueblo..............................910
Cocopah Tribe...............................646
Comanche Tribe..............................3,597
Havasupai Tribe.............................591
Hopi Tribe..................................9,199
Hualapai Tribe..............................1,498
Isleta Pueblo...............................3,110
Jemez Pueblo................................1,889
Jicarilla Apache Tribe......................2,269
Kaibab Piute Tribe..........................229
Laguna Pueblo...............................1,485
Mescalero Apache Tribe......................2,415
Mohave Tribe................................836
Mohave-Chemehuevi Tribe.....................2,981
Navajo Tribe................................165,065
Paiute Tribe................................412
Pascua-Yaqui................................6,227
Picuris Pueblo..............................177
Pima-Maricopa...............................16,465
Pojoaque Pueblo.............................78
Quechan Tribe...............................2,234
San Carlos Apache Tribe.....................10,120
San Felipe Pueblo...........................2,072
San Ildefonso Pueblo........................430
San Juan Pueblo.............................1,842
Sandia Pueblo...............................295
Santa Ana Pueblo............................501
Santa Clara Pueblo..........................2,327
Southern Ute Tribe..........................1,096
Taos Pueblo.................................1,860
Tesuque Pueblo..............................299
Tohono O'odham Tribe........................17,261

TRIBE	POPULATION
Tonto Apache Tribe	921
Ute Mountain Tribe	1,528
White Mountain Apache Tribe	10,147
Yavapai Apache Tribe	688
Yavapai-Prescott Apache Tribe	115
Zia Pueblo	584
Zuni Tribe	6,999 [157]

THE CEREMONY

The ceremony for healing is very complicated and yet, to a causual observer, it might seem to be unorganized. The majority of the serious actions of the ceremony take place inside the medicine hogan. The ceremony is moved from one home to another in some instances. The following simplified description of activities either have been observed at ceremonies or told to the author by Navajo friends. This description does not give the religious details for obvious reasons.

The ceremony usually begins about ten o'clock in the evening of the first night of the sing. The medicine man first sings a long series of prayers. A drum, made by inverting a basket, is played to accompany the prayers.

At dawn, the medicine man says certain prayers while he sets up a special religious symbol that he has selected for the patient. Later in the morning, a large fire is built in the medicine house for the patient, and anyone else who wishes to participate, to purify their bodies by sweating and using an emetic. The emetic is swallowed and rubbed on the body. Each person makes a pile of dirt for their vomit. This is carried out later and disposed of away from the medicine hogan. This activity lasts for an hour or more, depending upon the number of people who wish to participate.

The medicine man prepares prayer sticks. The patient holds a crystal up to the sun to signify lighting of the prayer sticks. The prayer sticks are then wrapped in a cloth and held by the patient while he repeats word for word the prayer said by the medicine man inviting the Holy Ones. The prayer sticks are then placed in a spot where they will attract the Holy Ones.

Approximately the same activities are repeated for three more days and nights. The songs become progressively longer as the ceremony proceeds and the prayer sticks are changed each day to attract different Holy Ones. At dawn of the fifth day, the medicine bundle is set outside the house and a special prayer is said by the medicine man to attract the Holy Ones until the sand painting can be completed.

The medicine man and his helpers then prepare the sand-painting, but not in the presence of the patient. The sand-painting may be completed in a few hours or it may take all day, depending upon the complexity of the pattern.

The patient is summoned into the medicine house and placed on the sandpainting. Most of the patient's clothing is removed and sand from the sandpainting, with other sacred objects, are applied to the body while the appropriate prayers are sung. This activity is completed in less than half an hour and the sandpainting is obliterated. The sand is taken out of the house and dispersed in a special place by one of the helpers.

Different sandpaintings are used for each of the next four days. They match the prayer sticks, made during the previous four days, to attract certain Holy Ones.

On the ninth day, the patient bathes his body and hair in the suds of yucca roots. The patient dries off with cornmeal as a symbol of future blessings. The medicine man paints a secret symbol from the sandpainting on the body of the patient before placing him on the sandpainting. The patient then becomes one with the Holy Ones.

On the last night of the ceremony, the patient must remain awake and pay close attention to all of the songs and prayers that summarize the events of the ritual which gives the ceremony its strength. This activity is continued until sun up of the ninth day from the night that the chant began.

As the patient leaves the medicine house he breathes deeply, facing the east, signifying the acceptance of the blessings from the Holy Ones during the ceremony. The patient may not participate in any usual daily activities and must stay awake until after noon. Then he may sleep.

The patient cannot comb his hair, remove any clothing or perform any work until dawn of the fourth day after the ceremony. During these four days, the patient must not touch anyone who has not had this ceremony. He still represents the power of the Holy Ones who attended him, power absorbed through contact with sacred objects and paintings on his body. Harm would come to the one touched by the patient because he is unprotected.

The medicine man gives the patient a small perfect turquoise bead and a small olivella shell bead tied with a short string. These are to be worn at all times by the patient, usually on the hair string for those with long hair, as an earring, or around the neck. In times of danger, the patient may use the beads to seek aid from the Holy Ones.[158]

APPENDIX D

1869 BIA   FT. DEFIANCE,AZ. ONE ROOM, TEMPORARY.

1870 BIA   FT. DEFIANCE,AZ. ADOBE BUILDING, TEMPO-
RARY.

1880 BIA   FT. DEFIANCE BOARDING SCHOOL,AZ.*
CHEMAWA INDIAN SCHOOL, OR.

1884 BIA   CHILOCCO INDIAN SCHOOL, OK.
HASKELL INSTITUTE, KS.

1886 BIA   ALBUQUERQUE INDIAN SCHOOL, NM. GRAND
JUNCTION INDIAN SCHOOL, CO.*

1887 BIA   KEAMS CANYON BOARDING SCHOOL, AZ.

1890 BIA   SANTE FE INDIAN SCHOOL, NM. FT. MOHAVE
INDIAN SCHOOL, AZ.* STEWART INDIAN
SCHOOL, NV.

1891 BIA   PHOENIX INDIAN SCHOOL, AZ.*

1893 BIA   FT. APACHE INDIAN SCHOOL, AZ.*

1894 PUBLIC   TUBA CITY ELEMENTARY SCHOOL,AZ

1895 BIA   TOHATCHI BOARDING SCHOOL, NM.* ONE
ROOM, TEMPORARY.

1898 BIA   BLUE CANYON BOARDING SCHOOL, AZ.*

1899 CHURCH   NAVAJO METHODIST MISSION SCHOOL,
NM.

1902 BIA   TUBA CITY BOARDING SCHOOL, AZ.-
SHERMAN INSTITUTE, CA.

CHURCH   GANADO MISSION SCHOOL, AZ.* ST.
                MICHAEL'S INDIAN SCHOOL, AZ.

1903 BIA   SHIPROCK BOARDING SCHOOL, NM.

    CHURCH   REHOBOTH MISSION SCHOOL, NM.

1909 BIA   LEUPP BOARDING SCHOOL, AZ*

1910 BIA   CHINLE BOARDING SCHOOL, AZ.* CROWN
            POINT, NM. PUEBLO BONITO, NM.

1913 BIA   TOADALENA BOARDING SCHOOL, NM.*

1925 BIA   FT. WINGATE BOARDING SCHOOL, NM.

1927 CHURCH   GOOD SHEPHERD MISSION SCHOOL,
                NM.

1935 BIA   DAY SCHOOL CONSTRUCTION: ANETH, UT.
            BACA, NM. COYOTE CANYON, NM. IYANBITO,
            AZ. KLAGETOH, AZ. LAKE VALLEY, NM.
            MEXICAN SPRINGS, NM. NASCHITTI, NM.
            NAVAJO MOUNTAIN, AZ. NENAHNIZAD, AZ.
            PINE DALE, NM. PUEBLO PINTADA, NM.
            RAMAH, NM. RED ROCK, AZ. ROCK POINT, AZ.
            ROUGH ROCK, AZ. TOLANI LAKE, AZ.TEEC
            NOSPAS, AZ. TORREON, NM. TWIN LAKES,
            NM. WHITE HORSE LAKE, NM.

1941 CHURCH   NAVAJO BIBLE ACADEMY, NM. NAVAJO
                GOSPEL MISSION, AZ. HARD ROCKS,
                AZ.

1947 CHURCH   NAVAJO MISSION SCHOOL OF SEVENTH
                DAY ADVENTISTS, AZ.

1948 CHURCH   IMANUEL MISSION, AZ.

1951 BIA   INTERMOUNTAIN INDIAN SCHOOL, UT.

    CHURCH   MENNONITE MISSION AND BOARDING
                SCHOOL, AZ.

1952 BIA   ENLARGEMENTS: HUNTER'S POINT, AZ.
            CHEECHILGEETHO, NM. PINE SPRINGS, AZ.
            KAIBETO, AZ. NAZLINI, NM. SANOSTEE, NM.
            MARIANO LAKE, NM.

    PUBLIC   ENLARGEMENT/CONSTRUCTION:
                SANDERS, AZ. GANADO, AZ. WINDOW
                ROCK,AZ. TOHATCHI, NM.

1953 BIA   TRAILER SCHOOLS: BLACK MOUNTAIN, AZ.
            BORREGO PASS, NM. JONES RANCH, NM.
            KIMBETO,NM. SANOSTEE, NM. CHILCHINBETO,
            NM.

    CHURCH   LYBROOK MISSION, NM.

1954 BIA   ENLARGEMENTS: SHIPROCK, NM. KAYENTA,
            AZ. KAIBETO, AZ. NAZLINI, AZ. THOREAU,
            NM. CRYSTAL, NM. GREASEWOOD, NM.
            STANDING ROCK, NM. STEAMBOAT, AZ.
            PINON, AZ. WIDE RUINS, AZ.

    BIA   TRAILER SCHOOLS: CANYON DEL MUERTO,
            AZ. COTTONWOOD, AZ. LOW MOUNTAIN, AZ.
            TACHEE, NM. VALLEY STORE, NM. WHIPPER-
            WILL, NM. BIGGS STORE, NM. INDIAN
            WELLS, AZ. ROCK SPRINGS, AZ. SUNRISE,
            AZ. TOHLAKAI, AZ. WHITE CONE, AZ.
            HATCH'S STORE, NM. MEXICAN WATER, NM.
            RED MESA, AZ. SHEEP SPRINGS, NM.
            SWEETWATER, AZ. TOCITO, AZ-CAIN VALLEY,
            AZ. CAMERON, AZ. COPPERMINE, AZ. COW
            SPRINGS, AZ. DINNEBETO DAM, AZ, GOLD
            TOOTH, AZ. OLJETO, AZ. RED LAKE, AZ.
            SAND SPRINGS, AZ.

    CHURCH   NAVAJO GOSPEL CRUSADE MISSION,
                NM. SACRED HEART ACADEMY, NM.

    PUBLIC   ENLARGEMENTS: KIRTLAND, NM. NEW-
                COMBE, NM. NAVA, NM. SHIPROCK,
                NM. THOREAU, NM. TUBA CITY, AZ.

1955 BIA   BORDERTOWN DORMITORIES: AZTEC, NM.
            GALLUP, NM. HOLBROOK, AZ. WINSLOW, AZ.
            SNOWFLAKE, AZ. RICHFIELD, UT.

     CHURCH   CROWN POINT, NM.

1956 CHURCH   ROUGH ROCK FRIENDS MISSION, AZ.

     PUBLIC   BLOOMFIELD, AZ-CUBA, AZ-RAMAH,
                 NM. CROWN POINT, AZ. TOHATCHI, NM.

1957 CHURCH   ROCK POINT MISSION, AZ.

     PUBLIC   CHURCH ROCK, AZ. CROWN POINT, NM.
                 TOHATCHI, NM.

1958 BIA   BORDERTOWN DORMITORY: FLAGSTAFF,
                 AZ.

     PUBLIC   CHINLE, AZ. KAYENTA, AZ. PAGE, AZ.

1959 CHURCH   RAMAH DORMITORY, NM.

     BIA   TRAILER SCHOOLS: JEDDITO, AZ. INSCRIP-
            TION HOUSE, AZ. COAL MINE MESA, AZ.

1960 BIA   ENLARGEMENTS: LOW MOUNTAIN, AZ. FORT
            WINGATE, NM.

     PUBLIC   LEUPP, AZ.

1962 BIA   ENLARGEMENT: SHONTO, AZ.[159]

(Construction and remodeling have continued for many of the schools in this
report. The purpose of this chart is to show the periods of dramatic expansion of the schools on the reservation. Although many of the original
schools are now closed, other new ones have been opened.)
‡ Facility Closed

DNA FOOTPRINTS OF THE NATIVE AMERICAN

MITOCHONDRIAL FOUNDING LINEAGE	LINEAGE DIVERSITY	DATE OF ARRIVAL (Years Ago)	MIGRATORY DATA

First Migration of Paleo-Indians:
Combinations of ACD.

A	.091%	23,000 to 46,000	From Siberia over the Bering land bridge to the Americas
C	.096%	24,000 to 48,000	Same
D	.053%	13,000 to 27,000	Same

ACD WEIGHTED AVERAGE 20,000 to 40,000 YEARS AGO.

Second Migration of Paleo-Indians:
B only Lineage.

| B | .024% | 6,000 to 12,000 | Not found in Siberia. From Eastern Asia and throughout Polynesia-to Siberia over the Bering Straight to the Americas. Possibly from Polynesian islands by boat to the Americas. |

Third Migration, Na-Dene Indians:
A only Lineage.

| A | .021% | 5,000 to 10,000 | Siberia over Bering land bridge to Alaska, Western Canada and North Westerm USA. |
| | | 1,000 | Na-dene migration to Southwestern USA, Navajo-Apache. [160] |

ENDNOTES

(1)*Treaty Between the United States of America and the Navajo Tribe of Indians, With a record of the discussions that led to its signing*, Flagstaff: K.C. Publications, 1968. 5.

This paperback booklet was produced as a part of the Centennial Year of the Navajos. It contains the pertinent discussions leading up to the actual signing of the treaty at Fort Sumner.

(2)Young, Robert W., *The Role of the Navajo in the Southwestern Drama*, Gallup: The Gallup Independent, 1968. 11-14.

This is an excellent source of historical information done by Dr. Young while he was an employee of the BIA. Much of his original research was accomplished when he developed the report for the BIA on the results of the special appropriations from 1950 through 1960.

(3)Young, Robert W. and Morgan, William., *The Navajo Language*, Salt Lake City: Deseret Book Company, 1962. 117.

(4)*Role of the Navajo.*, 3-4.

(5)Goosen, Irvy W., *Navajo Made Easier: A Course in Conversational Navajo*, , Flagstaff: Northland Press, 1968. xii-xv.

(6)*Ibid.*, 159.

(7)Yazzie, Ethelou, Editor., *Navajo History, Volume I*, Many Farms: Navajo Community College Press,1971. 5.

Ethelou Yazzie was one of the first Navajo teachers to have a distinctive career in the BIA.   She edited this work that describes the religious events that deal with the pre-emergence and post emergence events of the Navajo.   The colored illustrations are painted by Navajo artists.

(8)Wyman, Leland., *Blessingway*, Tucson: The University of Arizona Press, 1970.   16-20

(9)Reichard, Glady A., *Navajo Religion, A Study of Symbolism*, Princeton: Princeton University Press, 1970.   452-453

(10)*Navajo History.*, 83.

(11)Luckert, Karl W., *Coyoteway, A Navajo Holyway Healing Ceremony*, Tucson: The University of Arizona Press, 1979. 3-10.

(12)"*Proposed Findings of Fact in Behalf of the Navajo Tribe of Indians in Area of the Overall Navajo Claim,*" Docket 229, Volume 1, Findings 1-12, 1965, Photocopy.

This is a brief of the findings developed during the Indian land claims.   The portions dealing with the Navajo Tribe contain many historical facts.

(13)*Navajo Religion.*, 112-118.

(14)Reichard, Gladys A.,*Navajo Medicine Man Sand-*

paintings, *New York: Dover Pulications, 1977. 24-25.*

(15)*Navajo Religion.*, 48-49

(16)*Role of the Navajo,* 4-5.

(17)Squires, Sally, "'Ancient' genes may be key to Indian origins," *The Arizona Republic*, 12/25/90. B-12.

(18)Friend, Tim., "Genetic detectives trace the origin of the first Americans," *USA Today*, 9/21/93. 5-D.

(19)Underhill, Ruth, M., *The Navajos*, Norman: University of Oklahoma Press, 1956. 6-13.

(20)*Role of the Navajo.*, 12-13.

(21)Spicer, Edward H. *Cycles of Conquest, The Impact of Spain, Mexico, and the United States on the Indians of the Southwest, 1533-1960*, Tucson: The University of Arizona Press, 1962. 281-282.

(22)Forbes, Jack D. *Apache, Navajo and Spaniard*, Norman: The University of Oklahoma Press, 1963. 27.

(23)*Historical Calendar of the Navajo People*, Window Rock: The Navajo Tribal Museum, 1968.

The calendar was developed as a Centennial Year activity of the Navajo Tribal Museum in Window Rock, Arizona. The data was compiled by J. Lee Correll. The time period is from 1582-1962.

(24)Role of the Navajo,   10.

(25)Historical Calendar.

(26)Apache, Navajo and Spaniard., 103-105.

(27)Historic Calendar

(28)Apache, Navajo and Spaniard., 131-140.

(29)Role of the Navajo., 17.

(30)Apache, Navajo and Spaniard., 252-258.

(31)The Navajos., 58-59.

(32)Role of the Navajo., 90.

(33)Ibid., 18-22.

(34)Historical Calendar.

(35)Ibid.

(36)Ibid.

(37)Bailey, L. R. *A Study of Slave Taking and the Traffic in Indian Captives, Indian Slave Trade in the Southwest,* Los Angeles: Westernlore Press, 1966. 22-26.

(38)*Ibid.,*   26.

(39)*Historical Calender.*

(40)*Ibid.*

(41)*Ibid.*

(42)*Role of the Navajo.,* 27.

(43)Terrel, John Upton., *The Navajos, The Past and Present of a Great People,* New York: Weybright and Taley, 1970.   76.

(44)*Ibid.,*   96.

(45)*Historical Calendar.*

(46)McNitt, Frank., *Navajo Wars, Military Campaigns, Slave Raids and Reprisals,* Albuquerque: The University of New Mexico Press, 1972.   130-131.

(47)*Historical Calendar.*

(48)*Ibid.*

(49) *Ibid.*

(50) *Ibid.*

(51) *Ibid.*

(52) *Ibid.*

(53) *Ibid.*

(54) *Ibid.*

(55) *The Navajos.,* 115.

(56) Historical Calendar

(57) *Ibid.*

(58) *Ibid.*

(59) Bailey, L. R. *An American Concentration Camp, Bosque Redondo,* Pasadena: Socio-Technical Books, 1970.   131.

(60) *The Navajos, The Past and Present,*   174-183.

(61) *An American Concentration Camp.* 183-186.

(62) *Treaty.*   3.

(63)*Ibid.*, 5-6.

(64)*Ibid.* 9.

(65)*Ibid.* 18.

(66)*Ibid.* 18-26.

(67)*Ibid.* 3.

(68)*The Navajos, The Past and Present.* 208.

(69)Young, Robert W. *The Navajo Yearbook, Report No. VIII.* Window Rock: The Navajo Agency, 1961. 46.

The eighth in a series of annual progress reports for the Navajo-Hopi Long Range Rehabilitation Act, (PL 474-81st Congress).

The author covers the years from 1950-1960 but also gave history of each area. A comprehensive, professional report.

(70)*The Role of the Navajo.* 46.

(71) Hodge, Carl, "Politicans receive bad reviews in tragic story of Navajo relocation," *The Arizona Republic*, 4/19/81. A-10.

(72)*The Navajo Yearbook, Report No. VIII.* 377.

(73)*Ibid.* 384.

(74)*Ibid.* 385.

(75)*Ibid.* 374.

(76)Bommersbach, Jana, "Apache County--they do things their own way," **New Times**, Volume 13, Number 41, 5/19/82. 15.

(77)*Ibid.*

(78)Shaffer, Mark, "Tax ruling backs state over tribes; double levey awaits reservation firms, " **The Arizona Republic,** 4/26/89. B-2.

(79)Casserly, J. J., "Indians, modern times means old problems," **The Arizona Republic,** 3/5/82. A-7.

(80)Staff, "Navajo suburbia comes to changing reservation, " **The Arizona Republic,** 3/12/89. A-12.

(81)Shaffer, Mark and Trahout, Mark N., "Extravagance, hint of scandal mark MacDonald's leadership," **The Arizona Republic,** 1/15/89. A-1.

(82)*Ibid.*

(83)DeConcini, Dennis Senator and McCain, John Senator, "Removing barriers to Indian opportunities," **The Arizona Republic,** 3/5/89. C-1.

(84)Trahant, Mark N., "Indian Country, A year after senate investigations, reform is stalled--**The Arizona Republic,** 1/21/90. C-1.

(85)Manson. Pamela. "MacDonald aets 14 1/2 vears." *The Arizona Republic.* 2/17/93. B-1.

(86)*Treatv.* 21.

(87)*The Navajos,* 199.

(88)*The Navajos, The Past and Present.* 222.

(89)*Role of the Navajo.* 56-57.

(90)*Navajo Yearbook.* 1.

(91)*Ibid..* 19.

(92)*Ibid.* 65.

(93)Thompson, Hildegard. *Education for Cross-Cultural Enrichment, Bureau of Indain Affairs,* Lawerence: Haskell Institute Press, 1964. 15.

(94)Underhill, Ruth., *Here Come the Navajo,* Lawrence: Haskell Institute Press, 1953. 4.

(95)Office of Indian Education Programs, *Report on BIA Education: Excellence of Indian Education Through the Effective School Process,* Washington D.C.: Bureau of Indian Affairs, 1988.

(96)Kahn and Kahn Attorneys at Law., *"Analaysis*

of Navajo Education Authority," *Washington D. C.* : *9/14/81. Mimeographed.*

(97)*Report on BIA Education.*

(98)*Navajo Nation Education Policies*, Window Rock: The Navajo Nation, 1984. Mimeographed.

(99)Miller, Julie A., "Cavazos, Lujan Promise Focus on Indian School, *Education Week*, 4/5/89. 12.

(100)Rogers, Paul Brinkley, "Navajo Nation, Making Quantum Leap to Adulthood, Navajo suburbia comes to changing reservation." *The Arizona Republic*, 3/12/89. A-12

(101)*Ibid.*

(102)*Cavazos, Lujan Promise.*

(103)*Report on BIA Education.*

(104)*Ibid.*

(105)*Ibid.*

(106)*Cultural Values in Indian Education: A study of Parental Attitudes and Values Toward Education on the Navajo and Hopi Reservations.* Flagstaff: Southwest Behavorial Institute, 1971. Photocopy.

The public school districts at Kayenta, Chinle, Window Rock, and Tuba City contracted to have a

survey of parents who had students in the schools.
    The interviews were conducted personally by trained
district residents. The interviewers went to Flagstaff
and were trained in administering the questionnaires in
the language of the parents.

    It was a unique survey and the results indicated that
the public schools rated well with the local parents. Some
curricular suggestions were made and later installed by the
districts.

(107)McCowan, Karen, "Schools in Arizona get bad
report card on dropouts, funds." *The Arizona Republic,* 5/4/89.   A-6.

(108)*Navajo Nation, Making Quantum Leap.*   A-12.

(109)*The Navajos.*   60-61.

(110)*Ibid.* 61.

(111)*The Navajo Yearbook.* 152.

(112)*Ibid..* 152-153.

(113)*Ibid..* 154.

(114)*Ibid.*

(115)*Ibid.* 155-156.

(116)*Ibid.* 157-158.

(117)*Ibid.* 163-164.

(118)*Ibid.* 166.

(119)Donovan, Bill, "BIA gets Navajo OK to study overgrazing, Feed aid for tribe provides incentive," *The Arizona Republic,* 2/3/90. B-8.

(120)Thurber, Alan, "Tribes intensify business efforts for jobs, funds, *The Arizona Republic,* 10/16/88. E-1.

(121)*Ibid.*

(122)Thurber, Alan, "Plenty of workers are on tap," *The Arizona Republic,* 10/16/88. E-1.

(123)*Navajo Yearbook.* 67.

(124)*Ibid.* 81.

(125)Donovan, Bill, "Tribe to fight rowdiness at religious events," *The Arizona Republic,* 2/3/90. B-8.

(126)Rogers, Paul Brinkley, "Navajo Nation, Making Quantum Leap to Adulthood, *The Arizona Republic.* 3/12/89. A-1.

(127)Hodge, Carle, "Environment, lifestyles take toll on Navajo tribe, biologist says," *The Arizona Republic,* 4/25/81. C-12.

(128)*"Quantum Leap."*

(129)Donovan, Bill, "Beleagered MacDonald gets support from Indian activist," *The Arizona Republic*, 7/1/89. A-18.

(130)Editorial, "Indian activist. Revisiting Wounded Knee," *The Arizona Republic*, 7/4/89. A-5.

(131)Cheshire, William P., "Indians remain: let us not bury the past, but dig it up," *The Arizona Republic*, March, 1989. A-5.

(132) Donovan, Bill, "No space for burial of Navajos," *The Arizona Republic*, 10/1/89. B-1.

(133)Witt, Shirley and Steiner, Stan., *The Way, An Anthology of American Indian Literature*. New York: Vintage Books, 1972. 117-119.

(134)Farthing, David, M.D., "Racist remark unfair, " *The Arizona Republic*, 4/5/89. A-7.

(135)Rogers, Paul Brinkly, "Navajo Nation, `Making Quantum Leap to Adulthood," *The Arizona Republic*, 3/12/89. A-12.

(136)Cahn, Edgar, Editor., *Our Brother's Keeper: The Indian in White America,* New York: The World Publishing Company, 1969. 15-20.

(137)Willey, Keven A., "Easygoing Lujan enters fray as Interior secretary," *The Arizona Republic*, 3/5/89. C-3.

Zalbrod, Paul G.,   *Diné bahané, The Navajo Crea-*
tion Story, Albuquerque: The University of New
Mexico Press, 1984.   25.

(139)**Blessingway.**   46-62.

(140)**Navajo History,**   17.

(141)*Ibid.*   16-18.

(142)*Ibid.* 19-20.

(143)*Ibid.* 24-27.

(144)*Ibid.* 27.

(145)*Ibid.* 27-30.

(146)*Ibid.* 30-31.

(147)*Ibid.* 31-34.

(148)*Ibid.* 34-35.

(149)*Ibid.* 35-46.

(150)*Ibid.* 46-57.

(151)*Ibid.* 59-72.

(152)*Blessingway.* 574-605.

(153)*Navajo History.* 74-82.

(154)*Blessingway.* 461-492.

(155)*Ibid.* 1.

(156)*Navajo History.* 83.

(157)*Tribal Directory.* Phoenix: Arizona Commission of Indian Affairs, 1990. 6.

(158)The description of this ceremony is the result of many readings by the author, attendance at ceremonies, and information from informants. It is a simplified version, intended only to provide information.

(159)Thomas, Hadley A., *"A Historical Development of School Facilities for Navajo Children."*, Graduate Paper, Northern Arizona University, 1965.

(160)Data in chart extracted from: Friend, Tim, "Genetic detectives trace the origin of the first Americans," *USA Today*, 9/21/93. 5-D, and Squires, Sally, "'Ancient' genes may be key to Indian origins," *The Arizona Republic*, 12/25/90. B-12.

SOURCES

Bailey, Garrick and Bailey, Roberta Glen. *A History of the Navajos, The Reservation Years.* Sante Fe: School of American Research Press, 1986.

Bailey, L.R. *A Study of Slave-Taking and the Traffic in Indian Captives, Indian Slave Trade in the Southwest.* Los Angeles: Westernlore Press, 1966.

Bailey, L.R. *An American Concentration Camp, Bosque Redondo.* Pasadena: Socio-Technical Books, 1970.

Boas, Franz. *Introduction to Handbook of American Indian Languages.* Lincoln: University of Nebraska Press, 1970.

Bureau of Indian Affairs, *Report on BIA Education Excellence in Indian Education Through the Effective School Process, Office of Indian Education Programs.* Washington D. C.: 1988.

Cahn, Edgar S., Editor. *Our Brother's Keeper: The Indian in White America.* New York: The World Publishing Company, 1969.

Fisher, Stanley, A. *In The Beginning: A Navajo Creation Myth.* Salt Lake: University of Utah Anthropological Papers, No. 13, 1953.

Forbes, Jack D. *Apache, Navajo and Spaniard.* Norman: University of Oklahoma Press, 1960.

Foster, Kenneth E. *Navajo Sandpaintings.* Window Rock: Navajoland Publications, 1964.

Frisbie, Charlotte J. *Kinaalda: A Study of the Navajo Girl's Puberty Ceremony.* Middletown: Wesleyan University Press, 1967.

Goossen, Irvy W. *Navajo Made Easier, A Course in Conversational Navajo.* Flagstaff: Northland Press, 1968.

Haile, Berrard. *The Navajo Fire Dance or Corral Dance.* St. Michaels: St. Michaels' Press, 1968.

Hester, James J. *Early Navajo Migrations and Acculturation in the Southwest.* Sante Fe: Museum of New Mexico Press, Papers in Anthropology No. 6, 1962.

Historical Calendar of the Navajo People. Window Rock: The Navajo Tribal Museum, 1968.

Hoffman, Virginia. *Navajo Biographies, Volume I.*   Rough Rock: Navajo Curriculum Center Press, 1974.

Kelley, Lawrence C. *Navajo Roundup, Selected Correspondence of Kit Carson's Expedition Against the Navajo.*   1863-1865, Boulder: The Pruett Publishing Company, 1970.

Kluckhohn, Clyde. *Navajo Witchcraft.* Boston: Beacon Press, 1944.

Kluckhohn, Clyde, and Leighton, Dorthea. *The Navajo.* Revised Edition, Garden City: The Natural Library, Anchor Books, Doubleday and Company, 1962.

Locke, Raymond Friday. *The Book of the Navajo.*   Los Angeles: Mankind Publishing Company, 1976.

Luckert, Karl W. *Coyoteway, A Navajo Holyway Healing Ceremony.* Tucson: The University of Arizona Press, and Flagstaff:The Museum of Northern Arizona Press, 1979.

McCombe, Leonard, Voutht, Evan G., and Kluckhohm, Clyde. *Navajo Means People.* Cambridge: Harvard University Press, 1951.

McNitt, Frank. *Navajo Wars, Military Campaigns, Slave Raids and Reprisals.*   Albuquerque: University of New Mexico Press, 1972.

Native American Directory, Alaska, Canada and United States. San Carlos: Native American Cooperative, 1982.

Navajo Students at Risk, Navajo Area Student Drop Out Study. Window Rock: Platero Paperworks, Inc., 1986.

O'Bryan, Aileen. *The Dine: Origin Myths of the Navajo Indians.*   Washington D.C.:   Bureau of American Ethnology, Bulletin 163, 1956.

Powell, J.W. *Indian Linguistic Families of American North of Mexico.*   Lincoln: University of Nebraska Press, 1970.

Reichard, Gladys A. *Navajo Medicine Man Sandpainting.* New York: Dover Publications, Inc., 1977.

Reichard, Gladys, A. *Navajo Religion, A Study in Symbolism.*   New Jersey: Princeton University Press, 1970.

Russell, Ruth and Johns, Broderick. *Navajo Livestock Reduction: A National Disgrace.*   Tsaile: Navajo Community College Press, 1947.

Simpson, Lieutenant James H. *Navajo Expedition, Journal of a Military Reconnaissance From Sante Fe, New Mexico to the Navajo Country Made in 1849.* Norman: University of Oklahoma Press, 1964.

Spicer, Edward H. *Cycles of Conquest, The Impact of Spain, Mexico and the United States on the Indians of the Southwest,* Tucson: University of Arizona Press, Third Printing, 1970.

Terrell, John Upton. *The Navajos, The Past and Present of a Great People,* New York: Weybright and Talley, 1970.

Thompson, Hildegard. *Education for Cross-Cultural Enrichment,* Lawrence: Bureau of Indian Affairs, Haskell Institute Press , 1964.

Treaty Between the United States of America and the Navajo Tribe of Indians, With a record of the discussions that led to its signing. Flagstaff: K.C. Publications in Cooperation with the Navajo Tribe as the Eighth in a Continuing Series Commemorating the Navajo Centennial, 1968.

Tyler, S. Lymann. *A History of Indian Policy.* Washington D.C.: Bureau of Indian Affairs, 1973.

Underhill, Ruth. *Here Come The Navajo.* Lawrence: Haskell Institute Press, 1953.

Underhill, Ruth. *The Navajos.* Norman: University of Oklahoma Press, 1956.

Villasenor, David. *Tapestries in Sand, The Spirit of Indian Sandpainting.* Healdsburg: Naturegraph Company, 1966.

Witherspoon, Gary. *Language and Art in the Navajo Universe.* Ann Arbor: The University of Michigan Press, 1977.

Wheelright, Mary C. *Navajo Creation Myth.* Sante Fe: Museum of Navajo Ceremonial Art, 1942.

Witt, Shirley Hill and Steiner, Stan. *The Way, An Anthology of American Indian Literature.* New York: Vintage Press, Alfred Knopf Inc., 1972.
Wyman, Leland C.. *Blessingway.* Tucson: University of Arizona Press, 1970.

Yazzie, Ethelou, Editor. *Navajo History, Volume I.* Many Farms: Navajo Community College Press, 1971.

Young, Robert W.. *The Role of the Navajo in the Southwestern Drama*. Gallup: The Gallup Independent, 1968.

Young, Robert, W. *The Navajo Yearbook, Report No. VIII*. Window Rock, The Navajo Agency, 1961.

Young, Robert W., and Morgan, William. *The Navajo Language*. Salt Lake City: United States Indian Service, 1962.

Zolbrod, Paul G.. *Din hahan*. Albuquerque: University of New Mexico Press, 1984.

Unpublished Materials

By-Laws and Policy Handbook. Arizona State Board of Education/Vocational Education, September 23, 1985.

Cultural Values in Indian Education: A Study of Parental Attitudes and Values Toward Education on the Navajo and Hopi Reservations. Southwest Behavioral Institute, 1971.

Kahn and Kahn Attorneys at Law, *"Analysis of Navajo Education Authority"*. September 14, 1981.

Navajo Education Policies. The Navajo Nation, 1984.

Proposed Findings of Fact in Behalf of the Navajo Tribe of Indians in Area of the Overall Navajo Claim, Docket 229. Volume I, Findings 1-12, 1965.

Thomas, Hadley A. *"A Historical Development of School Facilities For Navajo Children"*. Graduate School Paper., Northern Arizona University, 1965.

Newspapers
The Arizona Republic

1981: February 18/ March 1/ April 12, 19, 24, 25/ May 1, 5, 8, 10/ September 12. 1982: March 5/ May 19. 1984: April 5. 1985: December 8. 1988: October 16. 1989: January 5/ February 9, 18/ March 5, 12/ April 12, 26/ May 5, 7/ July 1, 4, 8/ October 1/ November 17.

1990:   January 12/ February 3, 21, 25/ March 12/ July 18/ August 9.   1993:   February 17, 21/ August 9/ September 21.

The Phoenix Gazette

1989:   February 28.   1993:   August 15.

The New Times

1982:   May 19.

Education Week

1989:   April 5.

Special Resource for Navajo History

Correll, J. Lee. *Through White Mens Eyes; A Contribution to Navajo History; A Chronological Record of the The Navajo People From Earliest Times to the Treaty of June 1, 1868.* 6 vols. Window Rock: Navajo Heritage Center, 1979.

GLOSSARY OF NAVJO TERMS

The Navajo terms and location names in and around the Navajo Reservation are listed in the glossary.

NAVAJO NAMES	ENGLISH NAMES
agháál	Prayer stick
a/ch'¿'adeez'á	Male hogan
á/tsé asdzáá¿¿	First Woman
asdzáá¿¿ nádleeché	Changing Woman
á/tsé hastiin	First Man
be' eldíílastnil	Albuquerque, New Mexico
b¿¿h	Deer
bináá'yee aghánii	Monster That Kills With His Eyes
ch'óol'í¿'í	Precious Stones-Gobernado Knob
déélgééd	Horned Monster
dibé nitsaa	Obsidian Mountain-La Plata Mountains
dook'o'oos/iid	Abalone Shell Mountain-Humphrey Peak, Arizona
dzi/ ná'ood/ii	Banded Rock Mountain-Huerfano Peak, New

NAVAJO NAMES	NAVAJO NAMES
	Mexico
haashch'ééh dine'é	The Holy Ones
hajííhéí	Place of Emergence
hashtł'ishnii	Mud Clan
honágháahnii	One Walks Around You Clan
hooghan nímazí	Female Hogan
hózhóójí	Blessingway Ceremony
jóhónaa'éí hataa'lá	Twin's Father-The Sun
k'aa' dine'é	Many Arrows People
kiis'áanii	Hopi Indians
kinłání	Flagstaff, Arizona
naakaii	Mexicans
na'nízhoozhí	Gallup, New Mexico
kiyaa'áanii	Tower House Clan
naayéé' neezghání	Monster Slayer
nádleeh	The Hermaphrodite
séíł'áád	Moving Sands
shash	Bear
siláo	Police

NAVAJO NAMES	ENGLISH NAMES
sis naajiní	Dawn or White Shell Mountain-Blanco Peak, Colorado
té'é'í hastiih	Poverty
t'iisyaakin	Holbrook, Arizona
tl'éhonaa'éí	Moon
tó dísh'ii'nií	Bitter Water Clan
tó naneesdizi	Tuba City, Arizona
tsé bit'aí	Rock With Wings-Shiprock, New Mexico
tsé naagháii	Rolling Rock
tséghahoodzání	Window Rock, Arizona
tsoodził	Blue Bead or Turquoise Mountain-Mount Taylor, New Mexico
yáahí	Little-small
Yéiitsoh	Big Monster

Source: Yazzie, Ethelou, Editor, *Navajo History, Volume I* Many Farms: Navajo Community College Press, 1971

Index

A

Abandoned uranium mines, 167
Agency superintendent, 102
AIM, 171, 180
Alchesay, 170
Alcoholic beverages, 55
Alcoholism, 167
Alexander W. Doniphan, 60
American policy, 60
American traders, 93
Among the Holy Ones, 12
Ancestors' remains, 172
Anglo-Saxon, 56
Angora rams, 148
Animal guardian, 216
Antonio de Espejo, 38
Apachean, 5
Apaches de Navaju, 2
Apachu, 2
Appropriated, 56
Articles of the treaty, 84
Athapascan, 5
Attacked Fort Defiance, 67
Awatobi, 49

B

Baptismal records, 52
Bar-N Ranch, 96
Barbon, 65
Barboncito, 81
Bartering system, 53
Bashas, 156
Baskets, 219
Bear Springs, 62

Bear Springs Treaty, 62
Beautiful Mountain, 62
BIA Bureaucrat, 187
Bilingual education, 143
Birth rate, 166
Black Eagle, 65
Black Mountain, 63
Blessingway
        events, 189
        songs and prayers, 218
Bootleggers, 168
Boquillas Ranch, 96
Bosque Redondo, 69, 75
Boundaries of the four sacred mountains, 221
British mentality, 56
Brutal inhuman treatment, 78
Bureau of Indian Affairs, 184

C

Cabeza de Vaca, 34
California Volunteers, 71
Canyon de Chelly, 50
Captain A. B. Carey, 73
        H.L. Kendrick, 65
Census 1800, 53
Changing Woman, 189, 201
Chanter, 12
Chapters, 103
        Chapter House/Community Center, 107
        Chapter movement, 103
Charles W. Poston, 71
Chattel, 52
Charvis, 65
Chihuahua, 65
Child Born of the Water, 205, 207
Children's clothing, 129
Christianity, 57
Citizens, 55
Citizens of Mexico, 53
Citizenship, 55, 57
Civil War, 68
Civilization of the Indians, 119

Collaboration, 89
Colonel B. L. E. Bonneville, 66
        Christopher Carson, 73
        (Kit Carson, 147)
        Dixon Stansbury Miles, 66
        E. W. C. Newbury, 62
        Edwin Vose Sumner, 64
        John MacCrae Washington, 63
        Samuel F. Tappan, 81
Comancheros, 51
Commissioner Collier, 148
Commissioner of Indian Affairs, 91
Completion of high school, 144
Compulsory Indian Education Law, 121
Confrontation, 114
Congressional Medal of Honor, 170
Constitutional assembly, 104
Constitution, 55
Cost per pupil, 141
Cribbed log hogan, 48

D

Day school movement, 126
Dead avoidance, 17 ·
Deadly uranium dumps, 167
Delgadito, 81
Demographics, 183
Dentist, 161
Diarrheal diseases, 161
Diego de Vargas, 45
Dine bizaad, 5
Discharge, 76
Distribution of royalties, 107
Division of Indian Health, 162
Domesticated animals, 146
Dominquez and Escalante, 50
Dramatic health improvement, 166
Dress
        Navajo women, 46
        Puebloan women, 47
Drought, 152
Droughts, 92

Durango, 65

E

Education, 119
Elder statesmen, 179
Eliminating Navajo culture, 123
Emergency feed program for livestock, 153
Encinal, 50
Enemyway events, 189
Estimated population, 53
Executive orders, 96
External pressures, 113
Eyak, 5

F

Fear of termination, 185
Federal courts, 55
Female hogan, 195
Fernando de Arguello, 43
First New Mexico Volunteers, 73
First night, 217
First teacher, 120
Five point stock reduction program, 148
Forbidden to speak their own language, 120
Fort Canby, 73
        Defiance, 64, 120
        Fauntleroy, 67
        Lyons, Colorado, 76
        Sumner, 76
        Wingate, 67, 89
Fourth night, 218
Francisco Vasquez de Coronado, 35
Francisco Lyva de Bonilla, 38
Fraud in Indian Country, 115
Fray Marcos de Niza, 35
French, 51
From the Verde Valley, 39
From this day forward, 84

G

Gambling casinos, 157
Ganado Mucho, 73
General James Henry Carleton, 68
General Order Number 15, 71
General W. T. Sherman, 81
Gila Apaches, 50
Glottochronology, 22
Governor Juan Bautista de Anza, 51
        Mendinueta, 50
        Meriwether, 66
        Perez, 54
Grasshoppers, 92
Great sacrifices, 126

H

Haida, 5
Hashtl' ishnii, 215
Hatathli, 12
Health Centers, 162
Health Committee of the Navajo Tribal Government, 163
Held in slavery, 94
Hell's Gate, 64
Henry Chee Dodge, 103
Henry L. Dodge, 66
Hernando de Alvorado, 36
Holy Ones, 218
Home Mission Board, 123
Horned cattle, 147
Horses and mules, 147
Horses were owned by the man, 146
Hosea Miguel, 65

I

Imitation is the sincerest form of flattery, 181
Indian Agent in New Mexico, 63
Indian Reorganization Act, 104
Indian scalps, 53
Indian Self-Determination and Educational

Assistance Act, 139
Indian Territory, 57
Insufficient rations, 92
Isolation, 126

J

J. L. Collins, 66
James S. Calhoun, 63
James Sutherland, 81
Jesus Arviso, 81
Johnson-O'Malley funds, 137
Joint-use area, 154
Jose Largo, 62
Juan Bautista de Anza, 51
Juan de Orate, 39
Juan de Valdivar, 39

K

Kick-back, 116

L

Lake Powell Navajo Tribal Park, 107
Land grants, 50
Language family, 5
Largest employers, 154
Leicester or Cotswold sheep, 147
Little Colorado River Navajo Tribal Park, 107
Livestock, 149
Living conditions at Fort Sumner, 78
Long walk to Bosque Redondo, 75
Long-Range Rehabilitation Act, 128, 161
Lorenzo Hubbell, 73
Louis Merriam, 125
Luis de Rosas, 42
Luke Lea, 65

M

Magdalena and Ladron Mountains, 88

Major continuing problems of education, 134
Major Ed R. S. Canby, 67
        Electus Backus, 64
        J. G. Walker, 62
Majority of all bubonic plague victims, 167
Male hogan, 195
Malnutrition, 78
Manuelito, 66
Many Arrows People, 216
Median age, 166
Medicine man, 12
Merriam Report, 125
Mescalero Apaches, 71
Military-like discipline, 120
Missionaries, 57
Missouri Mounted Volunteers, 60
Mitochondria DNA, 23
Monsters, 200
Monster Slayer, 205, 207
Monsterway events, 189
Monument Valley Navajo Tribal Park, 107
Mormon holdings, 96
Mother's clan, 7
Mother owned the sheep, 146
Mountain soil bags, 220
        Making the mountain soil bags, 219
Mud Clan, 216
Muerto de Hombre, 93
Multiple taxation, 113

N

Nadene, 5
Narbona, 63
Native American Church, 165
Navajo culture, 169
        Division of Education, 139
        Economic Summit, 155
        Economy, 51
        Education Scholarship Fund, 133
        Emergency Education Program, 129
        Headmen, 60
        Jewelry, 169

         Livestock on Hopi, 98
         Nation Education Policy, 139
         Preference, 139
         Stock, 148
         Treaty of 1868, 84
         Tribal Chairmen, 108
         Tribal Council, 107
         Tribal Headstart Program, 132
         Tribal park service, 107
New Navajo reservation, 88
Next night, 217
No space to bury their dead, 175
Nomadic war addicts, 56

O

Occupational Governor Bent, 60
Oil was discovered, 102
Overgrazing, 153
Overstocked, 148

P

Peabody Coal Company, 156
Peace treaty, 58
Pedro de Peralta, 41
Penal system, 121
Per-capita income, 156
Peter MacDonald was sentenced, 117
Picuris, 96
Pneumonia, 78, 161
Pohoaque, 96
Preservation and development of Indian lands, 187
President Arthur, 97
Pueblo Rebellion, 44
         Second Rebellion, 53
Public Health Service, 162
Public Law 568, 162
Pueblo Colorado, 73

Q

Quonset hut dormitories, 126

Querechos, 2
Quievira, 39

R

Radiation related diseases, bubonic plague and
        streptococcal infections., 167
Raffaille, 65
Raiding and slavery system, 64
Ramah., 89
Range deterioration, 148
Rations, 89
Relieved of his command, 81
Religious zealots, 123
Relocated, 57
Relocation Act of 1974, 96
Reservation, 55
Reservations, 58
Ricos, 52
Ruins and archeological sites, 176

S

San Francisco Peaks, 171
San Juan Agency, 102
Sandoval, 64
Sarcillos Largos, 65
School board members, 138
School construction, 129
School opportunities, 133
Search for captives, 94
Secretary of Interior James Harlan, 78
Secretary of State Alarid, 54
Sectarian schools, 123
Selected delegates-Delgadito, Barboncito, Manuelito,
        Largo, Herrero, Chiqueto, Muerto de
        Hombre, Hombro, Narbona and Armijo., 83
Self-sufficient, 58
Senator James R. Doolittle, 78
Senseless slaughter, 150
Sergeant Ranch, 96
Shaman, 12
Sheep, 147

Singer, 12
Slaughtered goats, 150
Slave girl, 146
Slave fair, 54
Small stockmen, 150
Smallpox, 159
Smithsonian Institute in Washington D.C., 172
Soil conservation, 148
Soil erosion, 94
Solution, 68
Sovereign powers, 105
Sovereignty of the United States, 63
Spanish census, 53
Special grazing permits, 151
Special Grazing Regulations, 151
Special Indian Agent Julius K. Graves, 78
Special Navajo Education Program, 130
Special relationship Bureau and the Indians, 184
Special Select Committee on Indian Affairs, 115
Square houses, 46
Stephen W. Kearney, 60
Stock condition, 152
Streptococcal infections, 167
Sub-chiefs, 101
System for expansion, 96

T

Talking God, 219
Teacher salaries, 142
The Indians Water Rights Office, 186
The Relief Administration, 149
The reservation concept, 188
The U. S. Senate's Special Committee on Investiga-
        tion of the Select Committee on Indian
        Affairs, 183
Third evening, 217
Title XI of the Education Amendments Act
        of 1978, 139
Tlingit, 5
Tohono O'odham, 3
Tonalea, 216
Tourism, 156

Towaoc, 157
Trade Fairs, 51
Trailer schools, 129
Traitor Navajos, 64
Translation, 4
Treaties, 55
Treaty of Guadalupe Hidalgo, 62
Tribalism, 170
Tuba City, 96
Tuberculosis, 78, 161
Turnover in teacher personnel, 143

U

Unemployment, 169
Universal education, 129
Urban militant Indians, 170

V

Vaccinated against smallpox, 159
Venereal disease, 78
Verb Paradigm, 9
Vowels, 5

W

Wartime shortages, 126
Water On It, 217